NONONSENSE

INTERNATIONAL DEVELOPMENT

Illusions and realities

About the author

Maggie Black is a writer and editor on international social issues, particularly in the fields of children's and women's rights, and water and sanitation. Among her books are: *Water: A matter of life and health* (OUP India, 2005), *Water, Life Force* (New Internationalist 2004), *The No-Nonsense Guide to the United Nations* (New Internationalist, 2008), *The Last Taboo: Opening the Door on the Global Sanitation Crisis* (Earthscan 2008), *The Atlas of Water* (Earthscan, 2009), *Children first: The story of UNICEF* (OUP and UNICEF, 1996), and *A cause for our times: OXFAM, the first 50 years* (OUP and OXFAM, 1992). Maggie Black is widely travelled in obscure corners of the Global South, especially in Africa and Southeast Asia, working as a consultant for organizations such as UNICEF, UNDP, DFID, WaterAid, Anti-Slavery International, IPEC/ILO, SCF and Oxfam, and as editor of major UN studies and reports. She has also been a co-editor of New Internationalist, Editor of UNICEF Publications, and has written for *The Guardian*, *Le Monde Diplomatique* and the BBC World Service.

About the New Internationalist

New Internationalist is an award-winning, independent media co-operative. Our aim is to inform, inspire and empower people to build a fairer, more sustainable planet.

We publish a global justice magazine and a range of books, both distributed worldwide. We have a vibrant online presence and run ethical online shops for our customers and other organizations.

- **Independent media:** we're free to tell it like it is – our only obligation is to our readers and the subjects we cover.

- **Fresh perspectives:** our in-depth reporting and analysis provide keen insights, alternative perspectives and positive solutions for today's critical global justice issues.

- **Global grassroots voices:** we actively seek out and work with grassroots writers, bloggers and activists across the globe, enabling unreported (and under-reported) stories to be heard.

NONONSENSE

INTERNATIONAL DEVELOPMENT

Illusions and realities

Maggie Black

New Internationalist

NONONSENSE

International Development
Illusions and realities

Published in 2015 by
New Internationalist Publications Ltd
The Old Music Hall
106-108 Cowley Road
Oxford OX4 1JE, UK
newint.org

Third edition – completely revised in 2015.
Previous editions 2003, 2007.

Cover design: Andrew Smith, asmithcompany.co.uk

Series editor: Chris Brazier
Series design by Juha Sorsa

Printed and bound in Great Britain by Bell & Bain Ltd, Glasgow
who hold environmental accreditation ISO 14001.

British Library Cataloguing-in-Publication Data.
A catalogue record for this book is available from the British Library.

Library of Congress Cataloging-in-Publication Data.
A catalog for this book is available from the Library of Congress.

ISBN 978-1-78026-239-0
(ISBN ebook 978-1-78026-240-6)

Contents

Foreword

On the banks of India's river Narmada, where I write this, a battle has been raging between people and development. For the past 30 years, communities here have fought nonviolently against the destruction to their homes and livelihoods by the construction of the massive Sardar Sarovar dam. With the dam now at full height, we are still fighting on behalf of the hundreds of thousands of people who have been displaced by this and other large dams along the Narmada River. Thousands of families have endured the loss of lands and livelihoods, homes and livestock, with negligible compensation or support.

The long struggle we have waged in Narmada is part of a wider war against a perverted paradigm of development which is being imposed by means of an unprincipled, unscientific, and undemocratic process. India's National Alliance of People's Movements is championing the rights of farmers, slum-dwellers, fishers and others not to be arbitrarily dispossessed of their lands. We are one of many similar movements around the world – the Zapatistas in Mexico, indigenous communities in Bolivia, in the Amazon and in Canada, farmers in Korea, Mozambique, India and the Philippines, fishers in Japan. These movements do more than symbolize the profound resistance the prevailing development model provokes. They constitute a struggle on behalf of a different conception of what development ought to be.

The injustices perpetrated in the name of 'international development' are the starting-point of this book. I welcome this, for if more people understood the damage being done to people and natural systems, tragedies such as the one we have faced in the Narmada Valley might be avoided. People who depend upon the natural resource base are finding that it has been unjustly acquired, stripped from them, and its natural wealth commodified to serve the interests of a consumer elite. Lands, water and forests are harnessed for the profit and benefit of those with power to purchase and invest – nationally and globally. Local systems of government have been forced to 'adjust', in such a way as to intensify the pauperization of those who, in many societies, still represent considerable numbers – even the majority. People faced with loss of life, dignity and livelihood have no option but to fight for their survival. From the micro-level, these movements connect into a global action demanding a major transformation of what development is and ought to be about.

In this No-Nonsense book on *International Development* Maggie Black examines the idea of development in the post-colonial world, looking through different economic, social and political lenses in the search for a more just and sustainable model. But she never loses the sensitivity or descriptive power so often abandoned in analytical discourse. Those committed to the defense of the downtrodden victims of injustice and exploitation will welcome a perspective on this vast subject which places their predicament at center stage. I sincerely hope that this book reaches and informs a new section of thinking people across the world. Let as many of them as possible become not merely spectators of development and its consequences, but supporters of and even participants in the new politics of transformation.

Medha Patkar
National Alliance of People's Movements
India

Introduction

Over the years, what I have witnessed in villages and shantytowns has brought home to me the predicaments of those whose lives 'development' is supposed to improve. Here is an example. 'When I was a boy, the water-holes lasted all year round. Now they dry up long before the rains. When the rivers flowed, we used to go fishing. Now the fishing baskets lie unused. We walked to school through high grass. Now the cattle have nothing to eat.'

This picture of dwindling resources, shrinking livelihoods, and deepening water and food insecurity is from Namibia. But it could come from many dryland areas in Africa, and from crisis-ridden corners of India, Nepal, Bolivia, Peru – too many places to name. This is what 'development' has done for many once self-sufficient people. Yet magisterial UN reports produce ever more complex arrays of statistics to tell us that poverty is everywhere receding. Certainly many good things have transpired in the 'development' era: lower child mortality, fewer illiterates, smaller families, better disease control. Sometimes it sounds as if the residual statistics of those still living at the edge of survival – which remain huge – are merely an unfortunate incidental. That is far from being the case.

The destruction of traditional forms of livelihood based on the natural environment amounts in certain places to a creeping form of genocide. Yet the commodification and plunder of the commons – forests, rivers, lands, soils, water – and its accompanying pauperization, development's 'collateral damage', or 'friendly fire', carries on regardless. The benefits of the modern world that might cushion people's livelihood losses or assist their transition to an economically viable substitute are frequently deployed so as to destroy them. Something is seriously wrong.

There can be no recipe for development, only many potential recipes for different contexts. Yet the development industry advances as if the opposite were true. Some kinds of gadget, medicine, or piece of kit may have wide-scale application. But true development is about people, and social beings do not function mechanistically. There is no common prescription. To be of genuine use to people, development has to grow organically, building on existing knowledge and systems, and engaging empathetically with different ideas. Is this really so impossible?

My worst confrontation with development as destruction came in India's Narmada Valley, where huge dams have wrecked hundreds of thousands of livelihoods. Many, if not most, of the victims will never be properly compensated. This is one example of a process endlessly repeated in different forms all over the developing world. Instead of addressing the human issues involved, politicians and their allies tend to look the other way, blaming a scapegoat, even the victims themselves. And if violent displacements from land given over to plantations, mines or mega-projects are a starting point, hypocrisy is a characteristic of development in many other contexts.

The range of angles is limited. Others would emphasize different themes – climate change, trade, democracy – covered by other titles in the NoNonsense series. Constrictions of space required generalizations and syntheses I regret. Development realities are hugely diverse – which, in the end, is the best cause for optimism. Whatever the difficulties they face, some communities even in the worst situations manage to turn their contest with development to advantage. To them, the best of luck.

Maggie Black
Oxford

1 The history of an idea

The idea of 'international development' was invented in the post-War world to describe the process by which 'backward' countries would 'catch up' with the industrialized world courtesy of its assistance. Seven decades and much sobering experience later, the concept has spawned an industry of thinking and practice and undergone much evolution. However, the numbers of poor people in whose name the mission continues to be justified are greater than when it was invented, and in too many cases their deepening poverty stems directly from the havoc it has inflicted on their lives.

Where should we go first to understand 'development'? Let us start in the village of Maurunga in Chiure district, Mozambique. Over 170 households here who depend entirely on farming for a living have had their land taken away and cleared, to make way for a sugar plantation and processing plant.[1]

Legally, 'their' land was owned by the state. The river-valley smallholdings from which they harvested cashew nuts and fruits were coveted by companies offering deals to the Mozambican government. Like millions of hectares elsewhere in Africa, the land was designated 'under-used' because it was farmed by small-scale producers. The company given *carte blanche* to oust them was the domestic arm of Eco-Energia, an international green-energy company specializing in biofuels. Sandrina Muaco, once a successful cashew-nut producer, was given $664 in compensation for her house and six hectares of trees. Such a sum is quickly spent. 'I lost everything,' she says, her living standards having plummeted to sub-subsistence.

If rural smallholders all over Africa are facing a mounting tide of corporate land takeovers sporting a 'development' label, many of their urban counterparts are in a similar fix. Since 2004, Mumbai's slum-dwellers – who comprise 60 per cent of the city's population and occupy just over 9.2 per cent of its land – have been fighting eviction and destruction of their homes to make way for shiny new office buildings and apartment blocks. The metropolitan Slum Rehabilitation Authority (SRA), in charge of transforming Mumbai's *bustees* (shanty towns), a habitat made familiar by the movie *Slumdog Millionaire* and the Pulitzer Prize-winning *Behind the Beautiful Forevers*[2], is in the grip of a familiar Indian trinity: developers, politicians and bureaucrats. It repeatedly flouts its own rules and processes to favor builders rather than citizens, using strong-arm tactics and offers of better living space to flatten decades-old communities.

In April 2013, after slum-dwellers camped out on the Chief Minister's doorstep and activist Medha Patkar threatened to fast unto death, a temporary halt was brought to demolitions and negotiations opened. This led to the review of six SRA projects for corruption, ineptitude and failure to consult, and gained some legal recognition for the rights of *bustee* dwellers. But the process of contest and attrition is endless. Promises are lightly rescinded, rights are unenforceable at law, and any day the bulldozers may – and do – reappear. In May 2014, a further 130 families of *dalits* and 'toilers' (India's lowest of the low) had their houses demolished.[3]

Stories such as these abound all over the developing world. The process of globalization, with its fluid movement of finance and commercial opportunity to wherever the market dictates, and its indifference to inequality and social injustice, has multiplied their number in recent years.

Sometimes the human fallout of land grabs, mega-dam or canal construction, paradise resorts and game reserves, or the burden on ordinary society of hugely expensive projects – World Cup stadia in Brazil, for example – sparks waves of popular protest. The 1,100 dead and 2,500 injured as a result of the April 2013 collapse of shoddily built clothing factories supplying international brands from Dhaka's Rana Plaza caused international outrage. But most development-related destructions never see the light of international attention because they consist of unspectacular incidents where small groups with no power or voice of their own are swept aside.

Mega-project planning pays mere lip service to democratic consultation, omits adequate compensation for the displaced, and neglects environmental and health concerns, even though legal provisions may be met in nominal 'on paper' form. International investment – primarily from the private market, with official endorsement and a fillip or concession from the public purse – is invariably involved. Construction is accompanied by secrecy, deal-fixing, corruption and inefficiency – and dirt-cheap wages for site laborers. The nexus of money and power buys immunity, even when gross violations of human rights are reported.

The irony is that these projects are carried out in the name of 'development'. In many ways, they are emblematic of development – its symbols, its markers, its statements of faith; and its all-too-familiar white elephants.

The essence of 'international development' is that it should combat poverty. Yet many of the projects that exemplify development adversely affect poor people and inflict poverty on others who were not poor before. They do this in the name of progress, modernization and economic growth.

Developmental contradictions

Estimates suggest that 15 million people a year worldwide suffer forced displacement as a result of construction projects and land sequestration.[4] This compares with 17 million refugees, and 33 million people internally displaced by persecution, conflict or generalized violence.[5]

But refugees may one day go home. Those displaced by development can never do that.

Balakrishnan Rajagopal, a human rights specialist at MIT, has described these forced dislocations of people as 'development cleansing'. They also constitute ethnic cleansing in disguise, since a disproportionate number of the dispossessed – in India, Brazil, China or the Philippines – are from minority groups. No-one knows how many millions of people altogether have been displaced into poverty by large projects: they are systematically undercounted. The 'development violence' contained in industrialization and urbanization is becoming better acknowledged.[6] So are the organized assaults on activists, environmentalists and human rights advocates – as in Central America, where agents of 'development' routinely deploy hit squads, paramilitaries or police against the dispossessed.[7]

There are other dubious aspects of these projects. Many turn out to have been over-optimistic in their cost-benefit projections, and while they may corral rivers, generate power, and adorn hills and valleys with palm-oil trees and sugar cane, they also contribute to the load of debt under which the country staggers. As a result, extra national resources are spent on paying back creditors instead of on the education, health, water supplies, and livelihood support that ordinary people need.

Truly, development is a very contradictory affair if it reinforces the very poverty that it aims to eliminate. How can something pursued in the name of 'the poor', to bring about improvements in their productivity and lifestyles, be co-opted to discriminate against them?

At the start of the new century, after 50 years of growing global prosperity, 2.8 billion people worldwide were surviving on less than $2 a day[8] – a greater number than the entire world population in 1950. Fifteen years later, despite the fanfare of the Millennium Development Goals, things are no better: 2.6 billion people are now living on less than $2 a day – a sum worth less than in 2000.[9] These are notional statistics, not head counts, anyway. The 'global poor' exist as an undifferentiated mass of imaginary beings, a statistical construct composed of millions of very different life experiences, to whose productive activities monetary values cannot accurately be attached.

Millions of people in some very populous countries, notably India and China, but others such as Indonesia and Brazil too, have indeed managed to move off the bottom rung. Even in the poorest countries, infant mortality rates have dropped, life expectancy has risen, and literacy has spread. These genuine achievements are often translated into claims of 'world poverty' having been hugely reduced. But the gap between rich and poor is actually getting wider.

Sometimes, claims that things are getting dramatically

Wealth and poverty

Statistically accurate comparisons across time are difficult to make as definitions and categories have changed, but even allowing for discrepancies, the gap between the rich world and the poor world has widened dramatically.

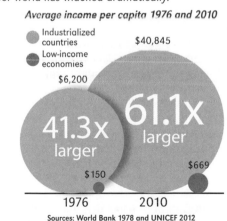

Average income per capita 1976 and 2010

Industrialized countries

Low-income economies

$40,845

$6,200

41.3x larger

61.1x larger

$150

$669

1976

2010

Sources: World Bank 1978 and UNICEF 2012

better because children are now vaccinated and succumb less often to disease, and life generally lasts longer, are not convincing. For example, in the midst of one of the vast shanty towns that compose 60 per cent or more of many African or Asian cities, where people's lives are a brutal, hand-to-mouth struggle inexpressible in standard economic nomenclature. Nor does 'a better life' defined in terms of reduced infant mortality make sense from the perspective of people whose homes and lands have been seized in development's name, and whose rights – sometimes whose existence – have been rescinded by bureaucratic sleight of hand.

In a world where extremists act out their hatred of the 'developed' in acts of mass atrocity, to say that the vision of 'international development' has soured is an understatement. The post-9/11 concern with 'terror', the backlash against Western meddling in the Middle East, the rise of China and its apparent engagement in the recolonization of parts of sub-Saharan Africa, have further complicated the relationship between the world's haves and have-nots. So have the escalating protests about globalization and environmental depletion, and the politics of people's resistance in settings where development has been experienced not as opportunity but as loss.

So is the vision of 'international development' a chimera and should the mission cease? If the activities carried out in its name are so fraught with contradiction and even constitute a pretext for violence, is the idea any longer useful? How do we come to terms with the reality that actions taken at the international level in the name of 'the poor' may do something for a country's balance sheet and some of its inhabitants, but nothing at all for those whose conditions of life justified it in the first place?

Beginnings

The idea of development was born not in the developing world, but in the West, as a product of the post-colonial age. Latin American intellectuals and leaders of independence movements – Gandhi, Mao, Nyerere – made important contributions. But its evolution in theory and practice has been driven by the industrialized world.

Today there is a large literature on theories of development, all grist to the mill of development discourse and proof of its academic respectability. Some authors seek the roots of the idea in Marx and Hegel, others go back to Adam Smith or the 18th-century Age of Enlightenment with its novel suggestion of transforming the world by scientific discovery and human intervention.[10] One or two even cite the dawn of agriculture 10,000 years ago as the moment the development train left the station.

Fascinating as are these philosophical excursions, for all practical purposes the international development idea came from US President Harry S Truman. On 20 January 1949, in his inaugural address, he declared that the benefits of scientific advance and industrial progress must be made available for the 'underdeveloped' areas.[11] The 1947 US Marshall Plan for economic regeneration in post-War western Europe had been a success, so something similar should be repeated in the rest of the world, to help prevent potential allies falling victim to the communist virus.

Within a decade, the East-West stand-off, and the accelerating departure of the imperial powers from their colonies in Africa and Asia, reinforced the strategic urge to lock 'emerging' nations all over the world into the US sphere of influence. Many newly independent countries tried to stay 'non-aligned', under presidents such as Nehru of India and Nkrumah of Ghana. This was the genesis of the 'Third World': an attempt to assert a group identity separate from both the capitalist West (the 'First World') and the Communist East (the 'Second').

As a geopolitical entity, the Third World never stood a chance. But that was not obvious at the time.

A post-colonial construct

As decolonization gathered pace, a new vocabulary was coined to describe countries emerging from a state of subjugation. The rush for independence – 17 countries in Africa raised their own flags in 1960 – put the seal on the construct of a 'developing' world, with which the Third World became synonymous. Apart from the geographical accident that placed almost all the new countries in the tropics, they had an obvious feature in common: their lack of industrialization – or 'poverty'. So what they needed was capital resources and technical know-how from the richer world in order to catch up. And if the First World was ungenerous, they would look to the Second.

Thus was born the push for international development, a concept which embraced ideological fervor along with more conventional notions of investment and technological transformation, and a vital part of whose impulse was the strategic and economic self-interest of the US and its allies. Countries that wanted to benefit from Western largesse adopted its language and ideas, swallowing any distaste they felt for the 'developed' and 'developing' dichotomy.

To offset overtones of paternalism, the global division was later reformulated as North and South. The notional lumping of countries together in large, essentially imagined, agglomerations was a holdover from the past. There had been the colonizers and the colonized. Then the wartime split of Allied and Axis Powers, then the East-West division. Why not a new dichotomy of 'worlds' based on a rich/poor, modern/backward version of reality?

The United Nations (UN), an inter-governmental membership body founded in 1945 in a burst of almost religious faith that international diplomacy and joint action could forestall future wars, provided a forum in which the new perspective gained strength. The UN's original *raison d'être* – international co-operation for mutual security – being stymied by East-West confrontation, it began to seek a broader mission: international co-operation for an assault on worldwide hunger, disease, illiteracy and all the economically and socially disruptive forces which fostered international turmoil.

The common mechanisms devised in the post-War world – the World Bank, the International Monetary Fund (IMF), the UN's funds and specialized agencies – helped confer on the development mission its international character, providing a set of multilateral bodies through which resources could be channelled. Other international groups of countries – the Commonwealth, the Afro-Caribbean Pacific states, and regional entities such as the African Union – later leapt aboard the development wagon, partly to justify or expand their institutional existence.[12]

Unfortunately, this proliferation of international bureaucracy and its accompanying propaganda has fostered the illusion that such a thing as 'international development' exists. It does not. Action at the international level is confined to a supporting role, providing funds and forums in which to carry on policy debates and undertake other exercises connected, sometimes tenuously, to what is happening to people on the ground. This reality is often ignored by enthusiasts who see international action for development as a be-all and end-all. Given the nature of power and its use by national and local rulers, this can never be the case.

The crusade takes off

The crusade began in the 1960s when US President John F Kennedy launched the UN's first Decade of Development in ringing tones: 'If a free society cannot help the many who are poor, it can never serve the few who are rich.' Whatever part was played by self-interest, there was also a heartfelt political commitment – not only in the US but in Europe and the Commonwealth.

The rich nations should help the poor – as Kennedy said – 'because it is right'.

Due to the growing power of media images, the public in the West became aware for the first time of hunger and suffering in large parts of the world. Shock that the majority of the world's people endured a fragile subsistence and frequent disease or natural disaster captured the public imagination. A powerful moral force was generated by the 'hungry millions' version of underdevelopment, nurturing a new breed of charitable organization such as Oxfam. Here was *the* post-colonial cause: the 'white man's burden' reincarnate.

The analysis was, however, simplistic. It was also confused. The victim of starvation due to drought or famine, and the farmer living in a pre-industrial society, were regarded as identical, and his or her image seen as the visual expression of the 'development' problem. But people who lived in self-sufficiency off land, forests, seas and rivers were not necessarily 'poor' – except in cash terms. In an industrialized world tuned to its own images of poverty, such niceties were buried.

The UN Development Decade set a target: every industrialized country should devote one per cent of Gross National Product (GNP) to Official Development Assistance (ODA) or 'aid'. Aid – transfers of public funds on concessionary terms – had previously only been associated with military or strategic alliances. 'Aid' was now to become the engine of 'development'. To many in the West, the idea was golden with promise. The post-War social contract was to be writ large on an international canvas and the world made more humane by rearrangements of wealth between the nations.

Optimism accompanied the launch of the development crusade to an incredible degree. There was a strong desire among progressives in the ex-colonial powers to expiate the sins of the fathers by helping to build a more equal world. From the new leaders of the South came an equally strong sense of urgency and commitment. Political and popular will were flowing.

Ups and downs

For a while, things seemed okay. Over the Decade, many developing countries raised their GNP per capita by five per cent or more. Unfortunately, any expectation that this might foster Western-style welfare states proved naive. The new wealth made little impact on the majority of people. An elite was becoming educated and 'modern', their fortunes and lifestyles integrated with the West. Meanwhile traditional economies became downgraded even as the numbers dependent on them swelled.

Lester Pearson, ex-Prime Minister of Canada, reporting on the 1960s Development Decade, commented that development could not be uniform for countries of disparate size, potential and existing organization; and that other characteristics than economic growth had to be considered: social progress, redistribution of wealth, efficient administration, political stability and democratic participation.[13] There is nothing new under the sun: these are the themes of much contemporary analysis. Pearson also presciently noted that the aspiration for development might be very different from the perspective of the poor farmer or urban dweller in Africa or Asia compared to that of planners, technicians and bankers devising policies on their behalf.

On the plus side, development's growing industry of governmental and intergovernmental institutions, university studies programs, specialist researchers, activists and charitable practitioners of every stripe generated a lively debate about the nature of development, how to make it happen, and on behalf of whom.

One school of thought attacked 'developmentalism', suggesting that poverty was structural and could not be defeated by the forward march of Western capitalism. Another rejected the assumption of power by large impersonal institutions in extensive areas of people's lives, with the proposition that 'Small is Beautiful'.[14] It was also suggested for the first time that there were 'limits to growth': that the planet's supply of non-renewable resources was under stress.

As well as generating a search for alternative development models, the debate prompted an attempt to argue the case for social investments as a vital contribution to, rather than a drain on, economic productivity. Various formulae were produced: 'Redistribution with growth', with an emphasis on job creation, and 'Meeting basic needs', with a focus on providing basic services. Even the work of small-scale development actors – charitable and humanitarian – became noticed and celebrated.

By the mid-1970s, the 'development' banner was fluttering over a diffuse collection of ideas and enterprises, and constantly expected to fly higher and wider. Population growth, urbanization, desertification, women's rights, ecological conservation: all were topics of major UN conferences, all were concerns the concept had to embrace.

Despite the critiques and questions, a spirit of optimism propelled the cause of development forward, not just among young radicals and progressives, but among the upper reaches of its own establishment. In 1973, Robert McNamara, President of the World Bank, called for the governments of the developing world to reorient their policies so as directly to attack the poverty of the poorest 40 per cent of their citizens, and the world's investment machinery to reorient itself to help them.

Also in 1973 came the successful Organization of Petroleum Exporting Countries (OPEC) cartel that hiked oil prices and held the oil consumers to ransom. It showed a Third World determined to extort more from the First and Second Worlds than the crumbs of aid rich countries were typically prepared to offer.

Buoyed up by this success, the Group of 77 – the developing world's organized expression at the UN

– made an attempt to exert some muscle by weight of numbers. Their high tide came with a call for a New International Economic Order (NIEO) at the 1975 UN General Assembly. No less a figure than Henry Kissinger, US Secretary of State, said that the industrialized world was ready to enter negotiations with the developing nations on a restructuring of global financial and trading institutions.

Sadly, commodity-based Third World unity was never repeated around any other primary product, and within no time the proposal for an NIEO sank below the international horizon. Instead, the surplus generated by the oil money bonanza helped to usher in the era of debt.

The concept starts to unravel

Ironically, the OPEC shock was the moment when both the geopolitical concept of a Third World reached its apotheosis, and the construct of a coterminous 'developing' world began to crack. The oil price hike produced a body of super-wealthy Third World states, while setting back development for others. How could the United Arab Emirates, with a per-capita Gross National Product (GNP) in 1975 of $13,000, belong in the same 'developing' bracket as Pakistan, with a per-capita GNP of $130?[15]

A number of non-oil-rich 'newly industrializing countries' also took on the coloring of developed economies. These included the four Pacific 'tigers' (Hong Kong, Singapore, South Korea and Taiwan); energy exporters such as the oil-rich in the Middle East and Venezuela; Thailand, Indonesia, India, Brazil and China. But in Africa, economies were in decline, food production was not keeping pace with population growth, drought and conflict were rife. A single descriptor for these many conditions as 'developing', not to mention any common definition of 'development', no longer made sense. No matter. The terminology and perceptions were indestructible.

Already splintering as a concept, the vision of world development receded dramatically in the 1980s. Recession in the industrialized world reverberated in countries heavily dependent on richer trading partners. In 1982, Mexico suspended interest payments on an accumulating mountain of debt, and sparked off a crisis of developing-world indebtedness. By 1990, total debt had more than doubled to $1,540 billion.[16] By its end, the decade had become known – especially in Africa and Latin America – as a lost decade, a decade of development reversal.

These were also the Reagan-Thatcher years, with the new orthodoxy of market supremacy, financial deregulation, shrinkage of government and the welfare state, which especially challenged the provision of healthcare, education, water, energy and transport by the agency of government. The use of public funds for investment in other countries' social and economic infrastructure was similarly derided.

With export earnings hemorrhaging away to pay their debts, many developing countries were forced to initiate 'structural adjustment programs' as a condition of IMF loans. Before long the enforced austerity and its human costs were prompting outrage in both North and South.

The new focus on 'non-state' and 'private' had one important spin-off. The importance of nurturing 'civil society' gained respect and the activities of a variety of non-governmental organizations (NGOs) were taken more seriously. Even if they operated on a localized scale, they were often effective service providers. And one thing they managed to do, which governments had not, was to reach the poor.

That development had failed the poorest was now increasingly obvious, whether at the level of countries, population groups or individuals. In Africa especially, an abyss was being created by the destruction of traditional economic systems and the failure to substitute viable alternatives. In international circles, there was talk of 'safety nets'. Except from NGOs and humanitarians, safety nets were conspicuous by their absence.

Internationalism redefined

The end of the Cold War, with its triumphant endorsement of global capitalism, was notoriously heralded by Francis Fukuyama as the 'end of history'. Euphoria greeted the prospect that the world could now enjoy an outbreak of international good will in which development could flourish.

The nature of the new world economic order was quickly revealed. In the words of social scientist Wolfgang Sachs: 'The events of 1989 opened the floodgates for transnational market forces to reach the remotest corners of the globe. As the era of globalization came into being, hopes of increased wealth were unleashed everywhere, providing fresh oxygen for the flagging development creed.'[17]

In counterpoise to the international market rush, there was also an influential rethink about what development should be about. From 1990 onwards, Mahbub ul Haq, an economist of world standing, began to publish an annual *Human Development Report* under the auspices of the UN Development Programme (UNDP). Haq set out to undermine the ascendancy of the 'Washington Consensus' that stronger growth and a positive balance sheet were the only measures of development a country needed.

Instead, human wellbeing was placed at the heart of the mission. This was to be measured by various social indicators – infant mortality, literacy, healthcare coverage, gender equity – as well as access to democratic participation and human rights. Results were combined with economic indicators in a composite assessment of progress. The goal of *human* development gave a positive impetus that carried through into the new millennium. And although the World Bank did not adopt human development as a lodestar, in 1999 it began reorienting itself by adopting the Poverty Reduction Strategy Paper (PRSP) process as the basis for country program partnerships.[18]

A new round of conferences under UN auspices – on the environment, human rights, population, women, food – provided settings where common commitment around policy directions suitable for the post-Cold War world could emerge. Although the release of ethnic and religious tensions previously held in check was leading to outbreaks of conflict in Europe and Africa, the development mission was reinvigorated. The UN presented itself to the world as an institutional context within which global anti-poverty targets and policies could be devised.

In 2000, this climaxed in a UN Millennial Summit and agreement to a global agenda of eight Millennium Development Goals (MDGs). These called for measurable reductions in extreme poverty and hunger, illiteracy, child mortality, maternal mortality, gender inequality and health-related targets for achievement by 2015. A tide of optimism similar to that attending decolonization had re-established the reduction of poverty as the key purpose of international development, and brought into being new 'global funds' and modalities for international assistance.

Other initiatives made progress. As a result of concerted campaigning on debt, 62 'heavily indebted poor countries' (HIPCs) received over $100 billion in debt write-offs and cancellations between 1990 and 2005. Strenuous efforts were made to slow the ravages of the worldwide HIV/AIDS epidemic, eradicate polio, increase child immunization and enhance malaria prevention. In 2005, at the Gleneagles Summit in the UK, came new commitment from the G8 nations to raise ODA budgets towards the now-accepted aid target of 0.7 per cent of GNP.

International development as a *cause célèbre*, glad-handed by such luminaries as Bob Geldof, Kofi

Annan, Nelson Mandela, Tony Blair, Bill Gates and Bill Clinton, was enjoying a global renaissance.

Contradictions

Not for 40 years was the international climate for a momentous push against poverty more favorable than at the new millennium. A cause that a few years before had looked to be in terminal decline suddenly regained worldwide political traction. And yet beneath the surface lurk many black holes and glaring dichotomies.

Apart from some exceptional 'failed states', most countries designated as developing in 1960 have become less backward, with some now belonging to the middle-income group and one or two joining the club of mega-industrialized global powers. But the catch-up has come at a price. The growing numbers of people in the South – at least 250 million in India and 800 million in China – who aspire to a Westernized lifestyle and can now afford a modest version of it, have joined a global consumer class whose appetite for cars, television sets, electronic goods, air travel, sportswear and fancy food requires the decimation of planetary resources and the near total exclusion of the poorest from meaningful access to any resource base at all. Over one billion people still languish in extreme poverty.[19]

When the development era began, governments were in the driving-seat and their actions and resources dictated the process. Today, states have ceased to be the arbiters they were. Corporate interests move freely across borders and the dynamics of globalized markets have taken over. The new transnational economic complex which governs the economic and social parameters of billions of people's lives does so with state compliance but beyond its control. Non-profit governmental and inter-governmental bodies such as those operating under the UN umbrella that might help offset 'development destruction' are, by definition, weak to the point of pusillanimity. Even many international

NGOs seem to be in thrall to globalization processes, seeking corporate allies and funds, copying their language and style.

Far from combating inequality, development has promoted it. A slew of recent economic analyses have shown that there has been a dramatic rise in inequality

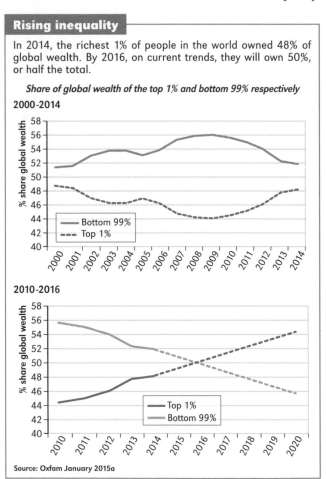

Rising inequality

In 2014, the richest 1% of people in the world owned 48% of global wealth. By 2016, on current trends, they will own 50%, or half the total.

Share of global wealth of the top 1% and bottom 99% respectively

2000-2014

2010-2016

Source: Oxfam January 2015a

over the development era, and that over the past decade the gap between the extremely wealthy and the rest has continued to widen. If the top one per cent fo the population owns nearly half the world's wealth, and is still growing its share (see graphs), not only do the poor have exponentially less but the entire development process must have blown off course. [20]

Regrettably, the globalization process 'is shaped by what political and social actors regard as just, as well as by the power of those actors and the collective choices that result'.[21] Extreme inequality, according to Thomas Piketty, is only sustainable because people are persuaded to believe it is justifiable. Therefore, despite its appeals to human rights and social justice, the contemporary crusade to end poverty has a synthetic character. It is powered to a considerable extent by smartphone products of the new world economic order in both North and South, and their quasi-corporate methods are almost as effective at ignoring those at the bottom of the heap as the globalization process itself.

Instead of a movement of solidarity with the excluded, members of the development set have moved 'upstream', claiming that advocacy for policy change is where most leverage can be exerted. An industry has grown up around 'objectively verifiable indicators' for everything they propose. Data collection, analysis and measurement substitute progress towards global targets for real improvement in people's lives. Development's standard-bearers are often more interested in generating and branding their products than in extending programs and services on the ground. One UK activist organization has distanced itself from this charade by dropping the word 'development' from its title.[22] Jason Hickel of the London School of Economics sees the development community as suffering an acute crisis of confidence due to the declining plausibility and imminent decease of the 'development' myth.[23]

When those who have been left remorselessly behind

in the development race are asked whether their lives are improving – an exercise which rarely happens because the results are too difficult to handle – almost without exception they say their situation is deteriorating.[24] Aid initiatives do not take into account their fears of livelihood loss, powerlessness, insecurity and family fragmentation. Instead, donors co-operate with state actions that deprive them of the resource base on which they depend. In their new post-development life, many such people will end up as lowly servants of others on a miserable daily wage, expelled to the margins of fruitful existence in the name of someone else's progress.

Proliferating development lenses

Despite the gloomy picture, whatever the record of development, this is not the moment to abandon the vision of a fairer world it was invented to create. If machinery exists to address 'global poverty', optimism insists that it be put to better use.

Over time, advocates of development have affixed qualifiers to the concept. One is 'human' development, a definition combining social and economic criteria for advance. Another is 'sustainable' development, embracing the need to conserve natural resources. A third is 'participatory' development, echoing the post-Cold War concern with democratization and rights. Finally, we have 'equitable' development reflecting contemporary concern with rising disparities and social justice. In the subsequent chapters of this guide, thinking and practice in such contexts are examined to see if they offer a route to reviving the vision.

There are other dichotomies to explore. One is the relationship between aid – or 'development co-operation' – and the process it exists to support. Is aid worthwhile? If so, for what kinds of activity? Another is the gap between things done in the name of 'the poor', and what they themselves value most. Their voice is insufficiently heard in the development discourse. What about other voices of dissent? Many observers salute the growth of people's movements against the homogenization of economies and cultures in a grand global corporate scheme as a manifestation of 'empowerment' and a rejection of the type of development that has caused so much pain. Others see it as a Luddite sabotage of the prescription for global success.

What is, actually, a 'state of development'? As a process, development implies change for the better – in the individual's circumstances as in society's. It is worth noting that humankind only started contemplating such a vision two centuries ago, and even now some societies still endure without any such aspiration. But change towards what kind of 'developed' society or person? The question begs others: what is the nature of the poverty this development is supposed to dispel? Many people living off the world's lands or forests without the benefit of modern amenities do not perceive themselves as 'poor'. Their aspiration is not necessarily a simulacrum of modern Western consumer society.

What then is the vision of the future to which the people in the village of Mauranga in northern Mozambique, or in the slum communities of Mumbai – the people themselves, not those who claim governance over them – aspire? Does it mimic or clash with the 'developed' life that those of us equipped to read this book expect to enjoy? And could any version of development be proposed which would keep a variety of dreams intact?

1 Hazel Healy, 'The smallholders' last stand', *New Internationalist* no 462 May 2013, p 12-16. **2** Katherine Boo, *Behind the Beautiful Forevers: Life, death and hope in a Mumbai slum,* Portobello Books, 2012; adapted for the stage by David Hare, opened at the National Theatre, London, October 2014. **3** NAPM, India, press releases of April and June 2013, and 25 May 2014, see napm-india.org **4** World Disasters Report 2012 – Focus on forced migration and displacement, International Federation of Red Cross and Red Crescent Societies nin.tl/disastersreport2012 **5** UNHCR Report for 2013, nin.tl/forceddisplacement **6** See, for example, Smitu Kothari and Wendy Harcourt in *Development* 47 (1), 2004, nin.tl/1BKNuDz **7** Martin Mowforth,

The Violence of Development, Pluto Press 2014, Chapter 9. **8** *Attacking Poverty*, World Development Report 2000-2001, World Bank. **9** *State of the World Atlas,* Myriad Editions and New Internationalist, 2014, pp 40-41. **10** Oswaldo de Rivero and others, *The Myth of Development*, Zed Books, 2001. **11** Gustavo Esteva, 'Development' in *The Development Dictionary*, ed Wolfgang Sachs, Zed Books, 1995. **12** See, for example, acp.int or the websites of the AU and other regional bodies. **13** *Partners in Development*: Report of the Commission on International Development, Praeger, 1969. **14** EF Schumacher, *Small is Beautiful,* Blond and Briggs, 1973. **15** Eric Hobsbawm, *Age of Extremes: The Short Twentieth Century*, *1914-1991*, Michael Joseph, 1994. **16** UNICEF Office of Social Policy and Economic Analysis, Memorandum, 28 June 1995. **17** Wolfgang Sachs, 'Liberating the world from development' in *New Internationalist* 460, March 2013. **18** See nin.tl/IMFfacts **19** Brian Tomlinson, in *The reality of aid 2014*, Chapter 4, nin.tl/realityofaid, p 134. **20** nin.tl/Oxfamonwealth **21** Thomas Piketty, *Capital in the Twenty-First Century*, Belknap Harvard, 2014, p 20. **22** In late 2014, the World Development Movement changed its name to Global Justice Now, globaljustice.org.uk **23** Jason Hickel, 'The death of international development' , Al Jazeera, 3 February 2015, circulated by Other News, english@other-news.info **24** Deepa Narayan, Robert Chambers, Meera K Shah, Patti Petesch, *Voices of the Poor: Crying out for Change*, World Bank, 2000.

2 Aid: the international contribution

Aid is the international arm of development. Rich countries have not been generous, but the key issues are to do with purposes and methods, not quantity. Aid has been heavily criticized, but it is spent on so many different things that it is impossible to take a definitive view about its value. Throughout its history, official aid disbursement has been driven by the donor agenda and relatively little has been used to address poverty directly; but without it poor countries and people would be worse off. Non-governmental aid also has its critics, but it does address poverty, supports alternative models and champions the dispossessed.

At the time when 'aid' was invented, the central role envisaged for it in development meant that instrument and purpose were seen as indistinguishable. Aid on a massive scale furnished by the industrialized world would fuel a 'big push', enabling development in poor countries to take off.[1]

This idea grew out of its predecessor: the Marshall Plan for post-War European recovery. But the situation in Africa, Asia and Latin America was quite different. In Europe, there had been huge destruction and human distress, but there was an educated population and know-how of all kinds. In much of the developing world, it was a question of building modern infrastructure for the first time, and there was no skilled or educated cadre waiting to run it.

It was clear from the start that aid would be used by donor countries for strategic, political and economic purposes. The question which failed to be asked was whether this could be done without compromising the fundamental intent. International assistance was seen as a bulwark for the wider pursuit of international peace and prosperity, and no contradiction was perceived between the motivations of givers and the interests of receivers.

The international mechanisms that had been resurrected or brought into being – the Bretton Woods institutions and UN bodies – provided channels for aid free of national self-interest. That the application of aid through them would cultivate allies and enhance Western interests was a given. Aid supplied through bilateral arrangements was even more unashamedly deployed to foster useful policy prescriptions, gain privileged access to natural resources and build markets for donor goods.

If the contradiction at the heart of the mission was not initially obvious, what quickly did become clear was that development, let alone poverty reduction, did not follow aid as night follows day. Many early ventures failed in spectacular fashion – such as an attempt to mechanize agriculture in Tanzania, Uganda and Zambia that left a trail of abandoned tractors.[2] Many attempts at modernization ran into similar disaster. Industrial plant and showpiece constructions fell into disrepair.

Development could not simply be slapped down upon pre-industrial societies courtesy of aid. Except for the colonizers' commodity extraction via mines and plantations, an autonomous modern economy and the institutions to run it had to be created from scratch. This was a task requiring generations, and how to speed it up by the application of aid has proved a puzzle ever since.

Although the Marshall Plan model was inappropriate, the concept remains iconic and new 'Marshall Plans' for Africa, Haiti and, most recently, the ebola-ravaged West African countries, are still called for today.[3] The idea that 'aid = development = poverty reduction' has proved so powerful that simplified equations about this causal relationship are repeated decades later without challenge. This does not help an understanding of what aid is or how it works.

Aid parameters

The justification for aid has always been poverty in developing countries. There is today a huge array of comparative statistics, much of the data collected and synthesized courtesy of – well, aid. This is most easily accessed via the World Bank's annual *World Development Report* and the UNDP's *Human Development Report*. Thus a 'world' picture of needs is compiled, to which aid is assumed to respond. But much of what donors do is unconnected to the poverty data – except that they pay for its synthesis and publication.

The early failure of the 'big push' for development was put down to the fact that the scale envisaged for aid or official development assistance (ODA) never materialized. But even if it had, the targets set – one per cent of industrialized countries' national income, reduced to 0.7 per cent in the 1970s – could never have accomplished the goal. The scale of aid is minuscule compared to the scale of 'underdevelopment'.

The idea that quantity is what aid is about, no matter what it is actually spent on, remains pervasive. Many donor programs still operate as if it was axiomatic that 'every transfer helps'. This has perpetuated an accountancy version of aid in which the donors' role is to check that sums provided are properly accounted for, not examine closely what they achieved.

Except among a handful of donor countries, the 0.7-per-cent ODA target has never been attained; total aid from the club of industrialized countries still averages just under 0.3 per cent of national income.[4] The most generous donors have recently been joined by the UK; the US gives less than 0.2 per cent. In 2013, ODA reached a new peak of $135 billion.[5] The global total amounts to less than the $164 billion (£110 billion) spent by the UK on its national health service in 2013-14.[6]

Approximately 10 per cent of ODA is for humanitarian relief in response to wars and natural disasters. In a

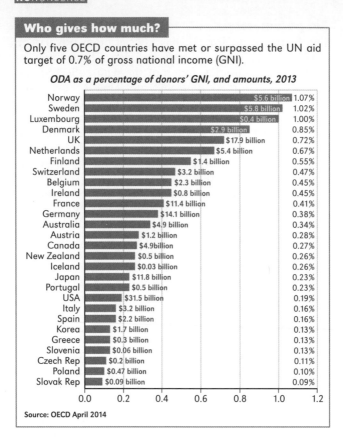

Who gives how much?

Only five OECD countries have met or surpassed the UN aid target of 0.7% of gross national income (GNI).

ODA as a percentage of donors' GNI, and amounts, 2013

Country	Amount	%
Norway	$5.6 billion	1.07%
Sweden	$5.8 billion	1.02%
Luxembourg	$0.4 billion	1.00%
Denmark	$2.9 billion	0.85%
UK	$17.9 billion	0.72%
Netherlands	$5.4 billion	0.67%
Finland	$1.4 billion	0.55%
Switzerland	$3.2 billion	0.47%
Belgium	$2.3 billion	0.45%
Ireland	$0.8 billion	0.45%
France	$11.4 billion	0.41%
Germany	$14.1 billion	0.38%
Australia	$4.9 billion	0.34%
Austria	$1.2 billion	0.28%
Canada	$4.9billion	0.27%
New Zealand	$0.5 billion	0.26%
Iceland	$0.03 billion	0.26%
Japan	$11.8 billion	0.23%
Portugal	$0.5 billion	0.23%
USA	$31.5 billion	0.19%
Italy	$3.2 billion	0.16%
Spain	$2.2 billion	0.16%
Korea	$1.7 billion	0.13%
Greece	$0.3 billion	0.13%
Slovenia	$0.06 billion	0.13%
Czech Rep	$0.2 billion	0.11%
Poland	$0.47 billion	0.10%
Slovak Rep	$0.09 billion	0.09%

0.0   0.2   0.4   0.6   0.8   1.0   1.2

Source: OECD April 2014

conflicted world suffering from climate change, these are on the increase.[7] The conflation of emergency relief with development assistance adds to the confusion over whether aid is philanthropic. Most development aid is not. Even humanitarian assistance can include security, law enforcement and infrastructure, involving expensive contracts with international companies.

Although it may seem niggardly compared to the scale of world poverty, aid quantity is far less significant than issues to do with quality. Aid has typically been used to help countries compensate for their underdeveloped status by tiding them over with advice, specialized expertise and subsidized contracts for high-tech investments. In the globalized economy, many consultancies and subsidiary companies have sprung up in North and South to take their cut from ODA largesse. The connections between these forms of aid and poverty eradication have always been tenuous.

A significant proportion of aid never goes near the South. It is spent on debt relief, research undertaken by faculties of development studies and other establishment add-ons in donor countries (a few are being outsourced to the South, mainly to save costs), as well as the towering edifice of international debate. A significant component of 'program aid' – that spent on activities in developing countries – goes to secretariats of donor-sponsored institutions.

A recent statement of the Organization for Economic Co-operation and Development (OECD) claimed that: 'The overarching purpose of ODA is to enable the realization of the human rights of populations most affected by poverty, marginalization and inequality.'[8] Over its history, the proportion of ODA that could genuinely be described as meeting such criteria is derisory.

The development mission

The invention of ODA had unlooked-for effects. It created a new subset of international affairs, in which developed and developing countries were cast as 'donors' and 'recipients'. Since the donors are automatically in the driving seat, this perpetuates an axis of superiority and inferiority. Some countries – India, for example – hate being cast as supplicants.

Another implication is that 'development' is only needed in poor, ex-colonial countries, although poverty is not confined to the South. And, in defiance of common sense, the idea is conveyed to donor populations that Southern poverty is so glaring that, unlike poverty at home, it is easy to solve by spending money on it.

In fact the process of intervening usefully in people's lives is fraught with difficulty. It is hard enough in one's own community; how much harder in societies with quite different political, social and cultural systems. Neat constructs of success and failure – which aid organizations are guilty of perpetrating – rarely apply. Donors refuse to admit this because it makes them look inept.[9]

The idea that aid is or could be instrumental in development has been extraordinarily tenacious; in fact, it has made a comeback with the Millennium Development Goals (MDG) agenda. This is because aid and the institutions associated with it, from the mighty international banks to the smallest charitable endeavor, are the principal international expression of humanity's global commitment to the common good.

But in the end, whether aid is effectively connected to development and/or poverty reduction is decided by

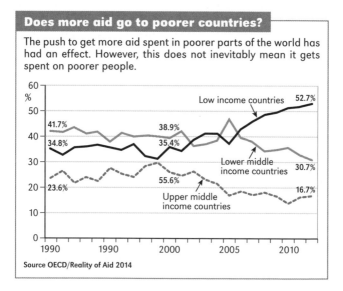

Does more aid go to poorer countries?

The push to get more aid spent in poorer parts of the world has had an effect. However, this does not inevitably mean it gets spent on poorer people.

Source OECD/Reality of Aid 2014

what happens on the ground. This is governed by the behavior of recipients – government and non-governmental. Developing-country bureaucracies typically suffer from shortcomings: lack of capacity, lack of means, lack of democracy, lack of efficiency and lack of outreach to the poor. These drawbacks are often overlooked at the donor center because they are so hard to deal with.

Development is subject to many influences, not all of which aid can or should control. Positive change can happen without the intrusion of aid, and much ODA has failed to make a useful contribution.

A range of critiques

Because aid was not the engine of development originally anticipated, it has come in for devastating critique. These come from both the ideological left and right, are often biased or poorly informed, and suffer from the problem of holding aid ransom to absurd expectations.

One school of thought derides all aid as damaging because it creates dependency, fattens bureaucracies and inhibits political dynamics in receiving countries. Others accuse aid of promoting an agenda that exclusively serves donors and the better-off, helping elites to feather their own nests, taking money from poor people in rich countries to help rich people in poor countries. Some critics, especially if they come from the South, manage to gain celebrity status even if their analysis is painfully thin.[10] Thus do some commentators eat aid's bread and shoot the hand that feeds them.

More standard complaints are that aid has often been filched or squandered. Some analysts have looked at the correlation between provision of aid and recipient countries' rates of economic growth and, finding no discernible connection, have dismissed aid as pointless; or, since they are themselves in the aid industry, have called for 'reform'.[11]

One influential treatise from William Easterly, an economist who spent 16 years at the World Bank, suggested that there was nothing to show for $1,000 billion disbursed since 1950 as living standards in much of Africa and South Asia failed to rise in 30 years.[12] He and the Zambian economist, Dambisa Moyo, choose to ignore the good things aid has done, and the fact that there have been many external and internal shocks – economic crises, wars, droughts, famines, HIV/AIDS, ebola – which aid has helped mop up. What would have happened without it?

The criticisms take in the nature and modalities of development, but much of the opprobrium is pinned onto aid. This is irrational. It proceeds from the faulty assumption that everything done with aid is the same. A question repeatedly asked is: 'Does aid work?'[13] The question makes no sense. 'Aid' is a gift or a transfer of resources on concessional terms, to be applied to improvements in wellbeing or productivity in developing countries. Apart from having this very broad purpose and a corresponding existence as a budgetary umbrella, aid has no generic character. One would not ask: 'Does investment work?'

The machinery of aid

The inter-governmental institutions – UN agencies, programs, funds, commissions and banks – and the bilateral bodies such as USAID and the UK's Department for International Development (DFID), are bureaucracies staffed by civil servants. Their common feature is that they spend money collected from taxpayers in richer countries in countries that are poorer.

Whatever the diverse members of this 'donor community' are most akin to – research institutes, consultancy firms, sub-departments of foreign affairs or boards of trade – they are in no sense charitable bodies writ large. The only exceptions are those with an explicitly humanitarian mission such as the World Food Programme (WFP), and bodies with a specific mandate for particular population groups such as the UN

High Commissioner for Refugees (UNHCR) and the UN Children's Fund (UNICEF).

ODA is formally channelled through governments. The donor-recipient relationship is conducted between representatives of donor governments (or UN bodies primarily responsible to donor governments) and their developing-country counterparts. Funds are applied to agreed purposes under the authority of ministerial departments and their personnel, sometimes with involvement from civil-society organizations. The layers of governmental and local involvement are often complex, and more of the aid is absorbed higher up the chain than lower down.

The degree of donor oversight varies from mere book-keeping, to careful monitoring of outputs and processes, to considerable influence at delivery level. The desirable pattern of these relationships is subject to constant debate. Too hands-off, and aid may be poorly spent or misappropriated; too hands-on and accusations of paternalism arise.

Since 2000, a new type of international player has appeared – the Global Funds. These are independent of government and mostly resourced by wealthy individuals and business corporations. The best-known, the Bill and Melinda Gates Foundation, has dispensed over $30 billion. The Foundation works with other aid actors including NGOs and through a range of operational partners.

Aid expenditures

Aid programs aim to improve technology and increase economic output in productive sectors; and fill gaps or expand outreach in social sectors.

Aid can be spent on equipment such as vehicles and IT, construction, and supplies such as vaccines, textbooks and tools. Material assistance may be imported, sometimes exclusively from companies in the donor country; though more effort nowadays is made to source local manufactures, which are otherwise undercut.

A great deal of aid today is spent on data gathering, research and assessment, responding to the demand for 'evidence-based' results. Other more ethereal activities have recently gained in popularity: advocacy, social marketing, communications and partnership-building. These may be intended to improve human wellbeing, but many are considerably removed from the coalface of productivity or service outreach.

Aid may also be used to pay civil-service salaries and departmental costs. This is often frowned on: governments cannot be independent if they do not pay their own staff. In some circumstances local government is perceived as so inadequate that donors prefer to set up their own project establishments. But these disappear when a project ends. If donors do not support local governments, they cannot gain capacity. The pendulum swings back and forth on 'budget support'; at present the tendency is to talk up the need for Southern ownership of development processes.[14] But the creation of checks,

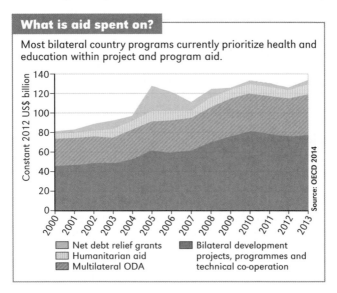

What is aid spent on?

Most bilateral country programs currently prioritize health and education within project and program aid.

Source: OECD 2014

☐ Net debt relief grants
▥ Humanitarian aid
▨ Multilateral ODA

◼ Bilateral development projects, programmes and technical co-operation safeguards and reporting systems can be a major absorber of donor funds.

Judgments about donor and recipient behavior *vis à vis* expenditures apply both ways. Southern governments may not be focused on poverty reduction as a priority; the projects they prefer are large-scale enterprises and infrastructure with few equity strings attached. Embedding poverty reduction in service delivery is a useful thing for donors to do. 'Capacity-building' can offset biases in favor of the better-off.

Technical co-operation

Around a third of ODA comes in the form of 'technical co operation': a euphemism for well paid experts whose skills recipient countries lack. These experts may be anything from hydrologists to epidemiologists, marketing gurus to statisticians, engineers to conservationists.

Although few spend much time in the field, their work may have a bearing on poverty reduction. For example, policies drafted may address health or other basic services, program processes may be designed to be inclusive, and projects located in poorer parts of the country instead of those favored by politicians.

An increasing number of technical experts come from the private sector. In conformity with the domination of neoliberal economic ideology, the role of corporate business in development is no longer disputed by the international bureaucracy; on the contrary, it is welcomed. Public-private partnerships – often a recipe for private profit by corporations and their allies, and public theft of people's resource base – have become ODA modalities. Private companies both give and receive ODA. For example, the Commonwealth Development Corporation (CDC) spends UK aid on gated communities for the wealthy, shopping malls and luxury property in poor countries.[15] This does not sit easily with poverty-reduction goals.

The large salaries and benefits enjoyed by expatriates paid from official aid attract much adverse comment. However, specialists employed by the donor community, including those from the South, are part of the donor economy and are employed at its – sometimes shockingly inflated – rates. It is an anomaly that the recent rise in aid budgets has inflated many donor-expert lifestyles to corporate levels.

These experts are primarily answerable to their donor employers, not to the societies in which they serve. This may be regrettable, but it is a fact. No government would be able to justify to its citizens an aid program over which it had relinquished control to the recipients.

The humanitarian players

Although inter-governmental aid may be inspired by humanitarian ideals, it is not normally designed to target people who are poor. By contrast, the non-governmental organizations (NGOs) have at their core the purpose of reaching the disadvantaged.

Such organizations come into being in direct response to human need and exist to address it. Their mandates are philanthropic, including efforts to address long-term poverty by means of development. Thus there is no confusion about whether they are targeting people or nations.

In recent years, the proportion of official aid given to and through NGOs has risen significantly. Many receive money both from governments and business, substantially supplementing income from voluntary donations. Between them, three of the largest international NGOs – CARE, Oxfam and Save the Children – mustered combined funds of over $3.2 billion in 2013.[16]

On their side, international organizations today raise money from private sources as if they were charities. UNICEF, for example, raises 25 per cent of its income from voluntary contributions.[17] All types of aid organization are becoming more like each other.

Many NGOs call for improvements and increases in ODA. Historically, this arose from frustration that the scale of their own efforts amounted to 'drops in the ocean'. Their belief that the way to make a significant impact is to make governments provide more aid has enhanced the confusion between aid with a human-wellbeing purpose, and aid with a nation-building purpose. It has also contributed to the nonsensical idea that development impacts can be 'scaled up' simply by making larger grants, and that there is something inadequate about saving people 'one by one'.[18] There is no other way to save people than one by one. By blurring the distinction between themselves and others, NGOs have done themselves an injustice. Their record in people terms is far superior to ODA's.

Not all NGOs are effective, many make mistakes and a few may be dishonest. But at their best they are in touch with the myriad realities of people's lives in a way undreamt of among the authors of the macro policy and the master plan. Some have helped find alternative models of development that better serve the poor, leading the way for government and international donors to follow.

The great aid debate

Whatever else aid has or has not done in the 60 odd years of its history, it has paid for a thorough debate about itself.

At key moments – for example, in the early 1970s, and following the end of the Cold War – there have been calls for aid to be redirected so as to achieve more for the poor. Aid has also achieved some striking successes: the transformation of agricultural technology and rise in food production known as the Green Revolution, and major advances in public health such as smallpox eradication.

Aid endured its most difficult passage during the 1980s when recession and the forces of political reaction punished aid. In the UK under Margaret Thatcher, the aid budget was only given the kiss of life when it was pointed out that it was useful for strategic leverage with allies, and that much of it went to the British development industry – UK companies, consultants and academic institutions.

For some years the idea that aid should primarily have a human-wellbeing purpose was eclipsed. The macroeconomic agenda known as the 'Washington Consensus' was promoted by the World Bank, IMF and the donor world. This was all about prudent fiscal and monetary policies, control of inflation, market supremacy, the reduction of the state and the slashing of social budgets. In a forerunner of post-2009 austerity in Europe, poor countries with balance-of-payments crises were forced into debt. The use of aid was subjugated uncompromisingly to donor interests.

This provoked a countervailing movement. Development and aid could not be co-opted so unscrupulously. A different kind of development was needed, one which emphasized investment in human and social fabric and refused to accept the high price extracted by market orthodoxy from the most vulnerable members of society. Thus was born the drive for 'human development' and 'justice', leading to the MDGs.

Push factors for aid

Campaigning efforts on behalf of international aid have to be set within the macro-political context. When the Cold War ended, great hopes were attached to 'the peace dividend' it would unleash for a new attack on poverty. But due to the end of aid as a component of Cold War strategy, budgets slipped downhill.[19] Other dynamics only began to operate post-9/11, when the climate for aid improved.

Suddenly, the consequences of extreme alienation associated with poverty became sufficiently threatening to impinge on donor minds. Recipient countries were quick to adopt the new rhetoric: 'To speak of

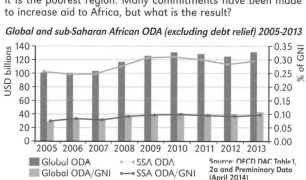

Is enough aid going to Africa?

Sub-Saharan Africa may not contain the most poor people, but it is the poorest region. Many commitments have been made to increase aid to Africa, but what is the result?

Global and sub-Saharan African ODA (excluding debt relief) 2005-2013

Global ODA | SSA ODA
Global ODA/GNI | SSA ODA/GNI

Source: OECD DAC Table1, 2a and Preminiary Data (April 2014)

http://www.one.org/us/policy/data-report-2014/

development,' said Alejandro Toledo, President of Peru, at the 2002 UN Summit on Global Poverty in Mexico, 'is to speak also of a strong and determined fight against terrorism.'[20]

The Summit, from which little was originally expected, produced new commitments to aid, especially from the US and the European Union.

The trend was strongly reinforced at the 2005 G8 Summit at Gleneagles in Scotland, when the raising of aid to $130 billion annually by 2010, coupled with debt-cancellation packages, was agreed. There were efforts to focus more aid on Africa, and less on countries which had achieved middle-income status even though – in South Asia, for example – they contain more poor people. Global poverty is now seen as concentrated in sub-Saharan Africa, but the rhetorical commitment to Africa has not actually translated into major changes in aid expenditure.

The positive aid climate which climaxed in 2005 was set back by the 2008 financial crisis and the downturn that followed. But continuing turmoil, with not only the

Iraq and Afghan wars, but conflicts in Somalia, Yemen, Syria and Libya, as well as natural catastrophes on an unprecedented scale, has kept aid budgets buoyant. The threat of terror driven by exclusion as well as fundamentalist belief plays a role in maintaining aid as a form of global insurance.

The involvement of new players, especially troops, in delivery of humanitarian aid has added further layers of confusion to aid's purposes and character, especially among recipients. Where once aid workers were seen as neutral helpers, they may now be identified as spies or Western protagonists and targeted for attack. The cause of polio eradication in Pakistan was compromised by the use of a bogus immunization team to identify the residence of Osama bin Laden, leading to vaccinator assassination. Aid workers in general, even those operating under the Red Cross or blue UN logo, can no longer expect protection derived from their humanitarian status.

Aid's use in the 'war on terror' has helped to maintain commitment, preventing – or masking – what might otherwise have been a collapse. However, the drastic diminution of the role of the state in underpinning human wellbeing and social capital in the US, UK and other European countries does not bode well for aid. If social benefits are cut at home, it cannot be long before benefits for foreigner populations, whose claims on 'our taxes' are disputed at the best of times, also suffer.

These and other dynamics surrounding aid today mean that it is undergoing change. In the effort to keep afloat in a highly competitive global world, and in the lack of distinction between its strategic and humanitarian arms, some aid appears to have lost its moral compass.

The expanding donor edifice

The growth in aid has encouraged the creation of ever more donor institutions through which resources can be spent. Unfortunately, many of these consist of extra layers of subsidiary donor activity. They try 'to make aid work better' on behalf of the poor by erecting machinery at the donor end. It is a sad irony that the expansion of aid has mainly fuelled the expansion of the aid industry, and that the poor make their principal appearances as photo-ops and human-interest adjuncts.

Along with an explosion in data collection and measurement associated with the MDGs, there has been a proliferation of new branches of development studies, more corporate NGOs, development media and publishing groups, research and advocacy operations, 'innovations' for development (mostly in communications technology), stakeholder conferencing and networking entrepreneurs. This expanding edifice of aid absorbs a high proportion of funds, moving the aid industry's center of gravity further away from meaningful engagement on the ground.

Today, the aid industry's principal preoccupations are centered not at the outreach level of programs and services, but several steps back and within its own apparatus. Working 'upstream' on policies and laws is presented as having a wider and deeper impact on the poor than engagement in delivery. This is a delusion: without practical assistance to make things work effectively on the ground, policies and legal obligations yield very little where it actually matters.

Within the UN system, there has been an attempt to unify operations in the name of cost-saving and non-duplication. The idea is that if goals and targets, planning, management systems, policy and best practice are synthesized within the 'one-UN' operation, roll-out on the ground will be more efficient. Since the industry measures its own performance and outcomes by its own criteria and tools, what this actually achieves for the poor is unclear. No system of feedback from their perspective has been built in. Instances can be found where, at their 'downstream' locations, programs generated by upstream activity cannot be found.

NGOs mimic the behavior and language of the

'professionals'. Their own dependence on government funds has led to their embrace in the donor fold and the anesthetization of their critical sting. In spite of long experience in the field, they buy into ideas that they know to be false – for example, that transformational change ('development') requiring the adoption of new beliefs, behaviors and practices can be speeded up and occur within a project lifetime of a few years.

They have also led the fashion for describing program results in value-for-money terms, implying that small material benefits can permanently transform individual lives, and that anything other than the expenditure of a few dollars a head is wasteful.

Some developments are, however, genuinely promising. Small, practical ideas that work – dry-season vegetables, micro-nutrient supplements, plastic toilet slabs and many other examples – can spread via smartphone technology at extraordinary speed. Microcredit and cash transfers enable people with minimal resources to adopt such improvements. Incremental gains in productivity may not show up in national tallies, but at the community level they are all-important.

The demand for 'success'

The contemporary donor agenda increasingly insists on evidence of aid 'success'. This has contorted the development process and led to a shift in focus away from program effectiveness towards aid compliance.[21]

The search for success is misplaced. Projects that can be fiercely criticized on one set of grounds may also have excellent attributes. Others that are impressive may collapse later because of a technical problem no-one could have envisaged. A classic example is the adoption of handpump tubewells as the main device for supplying village drinking water in Bangladesh, supported by UNICEF and other donors. When the water table dropped because sources were over-pumped for irrigation, arsenic contaminated the groundwater.

A program heralded a success for 20 years was roundly condemned. Yet no-one could have anticipated the arsenic problem, nor was the extraction of water for drinking its cause. No judgment about 'success' or 'failure' can be guaranteed over time, especially given constant contextual changes.

One critic of current trends in US aid describes a growing clash between the programmatic side of aid and the compliance side, whose agents he calls the 'counter-bureaucracy'.[22] These enforcers know nothing about development processes, especially those requiring decentralization of decision-making and local participation. Their chief interest is the avoidance of risk, the need to account for every expenditure, and the production of measurable results. The essential balance between these two components of aid, according to Andrew Natsios, has been skewed to such a degree in the US aid system as to threaten program integrity. Measurability may feed into 'evidence-based' analysis but have little connection to genuine transformations in people's lives.

Robert Chambers, a pro-poor development guru of long distinction, has echoed Natsios' critique in the UK, skewering DFID's adoption of 'payment by results' to govern its spending.[23] The perverse effect of deploying such an inappropriate managerial 'incentive' in complex settings is to destroy or bankrupt the most effective poverty-reducing programs. The over-riding aim is instant donor gratification. Nothing can be done at the slow, participant-governed, pace that real development requires.

Other commentators point out that 'evidence-based' analysis is often not the neutral, ideologically pure tool it claims to be. It can be highly deceptive when the so-called evidence comes not from concrete experience in the lives of the poor, but from synthetic constructs – average income, willingness-to-pay – that fail to take political realities into account.[24]

Next steps

At present, the international donor community is preparing to replace the MDGs with a new set of global goals. Already, this has generated an elaborate and costly exercise. On current intentions, in 2015 the UN General Assembly will declare 17 Sustainable Development Goals (SDGs) and 169 targets to be met by 2030.[25]

Whether or not the formation of the SDGs, and the subsequent campaign to implement them, will become the historic opportunity for the poorer populations of the developing world envisaged by some, the drive for better access to health, education, nutrition, clean water and sanitation needs to be supported.

Just as it is invidious to inflate the case for aid on spurious grounds, it does not help to seize on critiques of aid or questionable aid investments to dismiss the whole enterprise. The problem at the present time is that many of the important debates around aid expectations and practices are not being heard. The coziness of relationships within the donor community, and the echo-chamber world they inhabit, is dampening the voice of informed dissent.

The aid industry needs to recalibrate itself to listen to the voices of the poor, and to transcend pressures imposed by managerial enforcers who have no understanding of pro-poor development processes. If the donors fail to do this, some of those in the South who speak on their behalf will prefer to do without.

Aid is seen by them either as an outrider for damaging forms of globalization, or as a humiliating reminder of Northern ascendancy. Nepalese commentator Pitamber Sharma accuses aid of corrupting the minds of his country's bureaucrats, planners and politicians.[26] Naila Kabeer of Bangladesh would prefer aid to be limited to humanitarian relief, a position that many others would echo.

Their industry still being in the ascendant, the donors would strenuously resist such a move, and it is difficult to believe that declaring a moratorium on aid would, in the end, do much to benefit the poor. With all its contradictions and imperfections, the train will roll on.

1 WW Rostow, 'The evolution of the development doctrine and the role of foreign aid 1950-2000' quoted in Eric Thorbecke, *Foreign Aid and Development*, ed Finn Tarp, Routledge, 2000. **2** *Mwea: an integrated rice settlement in Kenya*, ed Robert Chambers and Jon Moris, Weltforum Verlag, Munich, 1973. **3** See reports on the establishment of the New Economic Partnership for African Development (NEPAD in 2001); Sam Jones on rehabilitation in Haiti, after five years of post 2010 earthquake relief, *The Guardian*, 12 Jan 2015; and .bbc.co.uk/news/uk-30995631 accessed 28 Jan 2015. **4** OECD, data on DAC aid for 2013, report issued April 2014, nin.tl/OECDdacstats **5** Claire Provost, 'Foreign aid reaches record high', *The Guardian*, 8 Apr 2014. **6** nin.tl/NHSkeystats **7** Brian Tomlinson, in *The reality of aid 2014*, Chapter 4, nin.tl/realityofaid, p 134. **8** Taken from the Statement of the OECD DAC High-level Meeting on Modernizing Reporting for Official Development Assistance, 4 Dec 2014, nin.tl/DACreportingODA **9** '£1bn spent to meet UK's overseas aid target', BBC news, 15 Jan 2015, bbc.co.uk/news/uk-politics-30843483 **10** Madeleine Bunting, 'The road to ruin', a review of Dambisa Moyo's book *Dead Aid*, *The Guardian*, 14 Feb 2009. **11** John Cassidy, 'Helping Hands', *New Yorker*, 18 Mar 2002. **12** William Easterly, *The Elusive Quest for Growth: Economists' Adventures and Misadventures in the Tropics*, MIT Press, 2001. **13** See, for example, Robert Casson and associates, *Does Aid Work?* Clarendon Press, 1994. **14** Tim Smedley, 'Shifting sands: the changing landscape for international NGOs', *The Guardian*, 28 Mar 2014. **15** Claire Provost, 'British aid money invested in gated communities and shopping centres', *The Guardian*, 2 May 2014. **16** Ian Brown, 'The company they keep', *New Internationalist* 478, Dec 2014. **17** UNICEF Annual Report, 2013. **18** See, for example, the website of the Children's Investment Fund Foundation, ciff.org **19** *The Reality of Aid*, Earthscan, 2002. **20** Charlotte Denny, 'World Welcomes Poverty Pledges', *The Guardian*, 22 Mar 2002. **21** Fenella Porter and Tina Wallace, Introduction to *Aid, NGOs and the realities of Women's Lives: A Perfect Storm*, Practical Action Publishing, 2013. **22** Andrew Natsios, *The Clash of the Counter-bureaucracy and Development*, Center for Global Development Essay, Jul 2010, nin.tl/CGDevel **23** Robert Chambers, *Perverse Payment by Results: frogs in a pot and straitjackets for obstacle courses*, IDS Sussex, Sept 2014 **24** Jan Vandemoortele and Enrique Delamonica, 'Taking the MDGs beyond 2015: Hasten Slowly', *IDS Bulletin*, vol 41, no 1, Jan 2010. **25** Ban Ki-moon, *Synthesis Report by the Secretary-General on the post-2015 Agenda*, nin.tl/BanKimoon **26** Pitamber Sharma, 'No pain, no gain', *Nepali Times*, Feb 2002.

3 Economic development – who benefits?

Development is primarily about economic advance, achieved in such a way as to eradicate poverty. But inequalities of wealth, within countries and around the world, are rising. Meanwhile the economies in which many poor people already live are ignored. Globalized market-led industrialization deprives such people of modest but viable livelihoods. Too little investment has been made in models that do not exclude the poor and would permit people living off the natural resource base or from 'informal' occupations at the urban periphery to gain security and a toehold on the modern consumer world.

Although the economic language in which they are described is universal, different people in different parts of the world live in very different economies. The task of development can be seen as linking these up – enabling those living in traditional or subsistence economies to join the economic mainstream.

After the Cold War ended and economic globalization took off, integration between the economies of developing and developed worlds finally began to occur. Much of East Asia, some of Latin America, and a few countries in Africa shed their underdeveloped status and hundreds of millions of people began to enjoy better incomes and higher standards of health and education. Development as 'catch-up' finally flowered and North-South economies began to converge.[1]

While economic globalization may have flattened out the difference between GNP per capita in West and East, South and North, and even led to the establishment of a new power bloc – the BRICS (Brazil, Russia, India, China and South Africa) – it has failed to do the same for people. Some have certainly gained, but many stay

Europe and America dominated the global production of goods and services from the beginning of the industrial era until around 2010. Their share has now declined to 50%, as Asia 'catches up' and is likely to drop further. However, Asia and Africa are still less productive per capita.

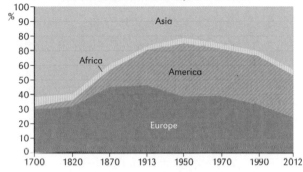

The distribution of world output, 1700-2012

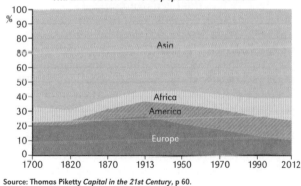

The distribution of world population 1700-2012

Source: Thomas Piketty *Capital in the 21st Century*, p 60.

behind, and others have been plunged into penury. In the enthusiasm for those the process has embraced, it is easy to lose sight of the fact that for those at the bottom, nothing has changed. In emergency-ridden or chronically unstable countries – Afghanistan,

Democratic Republic of Congo, ebola-affected Liberia and Sierra Leone, Central African Republic, South Sudan, and Syria among them – things for a large number of people have got worse.

Growing inequalities of wealth

Inequality is not a new phenomenon, even though it has recently become a *cause célèbre*, a pre-occupation of the global commentariat and world-class economists – such as Thomas Piketty and Paul Krugman – with no development axe to grind.

From the start of the development era, inequalities between rich and poor countries and people grew wider. In 1960, the income gap between the fifth of the world population in the richest countries and the fifth in the poorest was 30 to 1; by 1997, it was 74 to 1.[2] But when globalization got into its stride, the arrival of hundreds of millions of people, especially in Asia, into the outsourced jobs it created temporarily obscured the fact that inequality had not been overcome.

Those in the richer echelons of the newly industrializing countries, whose stranglehold on power and opportunity is pervasive, occupy a small economic plateau, usually gated, where they enjoy an automobile-and-verandah lifestyle. Linked into international markets and financial systems in the same way as counterparts in the Western world, the new global class has become increasingly remote from the slum-dwellers and village producers occupying their own backyard (except when they employ them as servants).

This polarizing process is happening everywhere, entrenching the rich and the poor in their social slots from Borneo to Bogotà, Kolkata to Cairo, Tegucigalpa to Timbuktu. Social mobility has ground to a halt, even in countries such as the US. Today, 7 out of 10 people live in countries where the gap between rich and poor is wider than it was 30 years ago. Most of the extremely poor live in what are now middle-income countries, with India containing more people surviving on less than $1.25 a day than the whole of sub-Saharan Africa. In Africa numbers are rising, even where economies are doing well. In Zambia, GDP per capita has been growing impressively, but the proportion of those living in penury grew from 64 per cent of the population to 73 per cent between 2003 and 2010.[3]

A tiny elite has become stratospherically wealthy: in 2014, according to Oxfam, the 85 richest people on the planet owned as much as the poorest half of humanity. But although this figure is highly arresting, illustrating the 'trickle-up' effect of uncontrolled capitalist dynamics, the gaps at the lowest end of society between the lower middle class, the just-about employed and the rock-bottom rest are ultimately more significant. The globalized economy has very little to offer to someone dependent on herding goats or scavenging plastic bags.

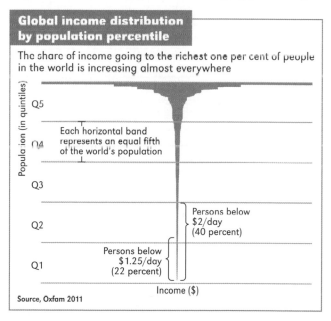

Global income distribution by population percentile

The share of income going to the richest one per cent of people in the world is increasing almost everywhere

Population (in quintiles)

Q5

Q4 Each horizontal band represents an equal fifth of the world's population

Q3

Q2 Persons below $2/day (40 percent)

Q1 Persons below $1.25/day (22 percent)

Income ($)

Source, Oxfam 2011

Mathematical poverty

Despite acrobatic contortions to make the statistics of poverty sound as if they are improving – the MDG of halving extreme poverty by 2015 is supposedly met – the reality is different. Visit a slum in Kinshasa, Lahore, Monrovia or Port au Prince, or a site where people are being evicted from their homes and lands, and the degradation and brutality of poverty is tangible. No statistics can do it justice.

Here they are, nonetheless. Around 40 per cent of the people in the South – 2.6 billion – live on less than $2 a day. Two-thirds, or 3.9 billion people, live on less than $4 a day.[4] A billion people still live in extreme poverty, on less than $1.25 a day.

These figures are constructs derived from mathematical formulae based on population figures, purchasing power, dollar equivalents and other variables. Their assumptions are arbitrary; the World Bank's $2 a day poverty line is less than one-fifth of that applied in the US and Europe. But they are the only estimates we have of the numbers of people still outside the modern economy or surviving at its edges. The development industry has recently made a fetish out of mathematical poverty, calling for an end to 'extreme poverty' by 2030. How on earth could attainment – even mathematically – be proved? The numbers are a delusion.

Millions of people find their livelihoods have dwindled or been swept away by the economic mainstream. Many victims of exclusion live in environments driven to collapse by years of political and economic adversity. Take the villagers of Siya Sang, a community perched in the steep canyons of Jawand district in Afghanistan. After 23 years of war and four of drought, a father, Rahim Dad, was forced to sell his only remaining asset, his 12-year-old daughter, into marriage for $80 to feed his family.[5] Her fate is not uncommon in an area where hunger is rife, tuberculosis rages and all other available assets – donkeys, goats, oxen, family treasures – have

Lies and poverty statistics

There is nothing reliable about the statistics of global poverty – neither the numbers nor the global poverty line(s). One problem is that the line is based on purchasing power parity (PPP) across borders. A drop in the price of, say, airfares in India may raise Indians' purchasing power and lead to a reported decline in poverty, even though the poor never buy a plane ticket. It is unrealistic to use one indicator sum across all countries anyway: poverty is relative and poverty lines in affluent countries are set far higher. In addition, a dollar indicator based on market values in societies where many goods and services are neither monetized nor purchased is notional in settings inhabited by many poor people. A number of recent studies have criticized World Bank methodologies surrounding the 'bottom billion' and '$1.25 a day' – the benchmark currently used to define extreme poverty. These calculations tend both to underestimate poverty's extent, and to overestimate progress in its reduction.

See: Sanjay G Reddy and Thomas Pogge, *How Not to Count the Poor,* 2009
nin.tl/hownottocountthepoor

perished or been sold already. In the failed economy of the failed state, the only marketable item left may be the servitude of children.

Transactions of this kind – trading girls into marriage occurs frequently in many parts of Asia and Africa, and increases when families are in situations of extreme vulnerability, such as refugee camps – do not show up in standard economic analysis. Nor do millions of others on which the people living in these economies depend, not to mention inputs to the household economy which are 'free' because they are gathered from the environment: water, food, fuel, fodder, housing materials, medicinal plants.

The one billion people surviving on less than $1.25 a day are kept alive by these contributions and transactions. That statement is itself an artificial monetization of livelihoods in an economy where cash transactions via a recognized market are only one, and may not be the most significant, lubricant from the perspective of those dependent upon it.[6] These economies are invisible to planners and treated by them as if they do not exist. Where they get in the way, they are routinely removed.

Invisible economies

Within these economic set-ups, the picture is far from uniform. The local setting and the dynamics of demand and supply within it, as well as social and cultural codes, affect livelihood arrangements. But in most of their settings today the picture is one of shrinking margins, greater insecurity, the breakdown of traditional social cohesion and increasing difficulty in managing assets of land, water, fuel, grazing and holding onto household reserves such as jewelry and keepsakes.

In rural areas, access to land is key. A family of *adivasis* (indigenous people) living on the Narmada River in Madhya Pradesh, India, might graze cattle in the forest, plant crops seasonally in the riverbed and lead a comfortable life. When a dam is built and the forest and riverbed are submerged, they become destitute. The cash passing through their hands when they were well off may not alter substantially. Since they never 'owned' land or had title, their economic status may be formally the same. But the livelihood base that they are forced to resort to – the unskilled labor of men gone to town, the scavenging of women – can barely support life. 'Now we eat only the cheapest rice, no pulse, no vegetables, maybe some forest leaves.' And before the submergence? '*Roti* (bread), *dal* (lentils), curds, rice, vegetables, fruits, everything.'[7]

India may have millions of new members of the middle classes, and high economic growth rates. But that does not necessarily benefit the people living in its many invisible economies. In several respects, comments writer Sunil Khilnani, 'India's new class of historically poor strivers have been forced to go it alone – while trying to negotiate an economy more volatile than ever, and just as corrupt.'[8] He sees the non-elite as even more vulnerable to decisions invisible and utterly unfathomable to them – 'decisions taken in the richest strata of the global economy'.

In India's most 'backward' regions, and in many similar environments elsewhere, the state barely exists except to permit its agents and private contractors to engage in resource theft. For example, the coal that lies beneath the soil in large parts of India – soil whose fruits maintain the lives of indigenous people. A 2013 Supreme Court decision threw out 200 coalmine allocations awarded to booming Indian companies by previous governments because of corruption allegations. But they are now up for sale again under the government of Narendra Modi, who is set to turn large areas of forest and *adivasi* lands into vast opencast mines.[9]

A British Raj land acquisition act of 1894, under which inhabitants of land wanted by the state could be arbitrarily evicted, was finally repealed in 2013. Its replacement ensured local consultation and certain standards of compensation and resettlement. But Modi's government has introduced a Land Ordinance to overrule the consent components of the new law.[10] Since no compensation package in India is ever delivered free from corruption, mines, dams and foreign capital are set to rule okay.

Indicators with a difference

Resource-base shrinkage is common throughout the South under the weight of economic, political, demographic and environmental pressures. It is reinforced in many parts of Africa where land is described as 'under-used' when it is producing for its small farmers a modest but adequate livelihood. Farmers usually have to scrimp in certain seasons if their cash crop does not do well. But if their 'under-used' holding is hived off to corporate investors, they will scrimp and go hungry all year round. According to Lester Brown, a pioneering environmentalist, for the first time in his long career, tens of millions of people in countries such as India, Nigeria, Pakistan and Peru can afford to eat only five days a week.[11]

While foreign interests take over 3.6 million hectares in Ethiopia, Malawi promises to set aside 200,000 hectares of prime land for commercial investors, and scores of thousands more are leased to foreign companies in Cameroon, Liberia, Honduras, Ghana and Cambodia, the rural economy in which small farmers have been managing to survive is air-brushed away or forced into liquidation. Traces of it turn up fleetingly, in the interstices of crop production or cattle sales, or in the mounting costs to national health or municipal budgets of high epidemic disease tolls or urban crime. They can also be detected in the statistics of economic migration, illegal urban settlement, the numbers of abandoned and widowed women 'heads of household' and growing numbers of children scrounging a living on the streets.

These are economic indicators too, but they tend to be seen as social outcomes of something called poverty, not as measures of poverty itself. And they are difficult to count: they occur in black, or grey, or hidden zones of economic life. As do the growing numbers of young women – in West Africa, Burma, Thailand and eastern Europe – being traded into prostitution or domestic service abroad. One of the most shocking characteristics of livelihood shrinkage is the way it has led to increased commodification of women's and girls' nurturing, child-bearing and sexual capacities – resources at the bottom of humanity's barrel when there is nothing else to scrape.

The growth question

At development's birth in the 1950s, economic growth was its essence. Today, the need for growth and at what rate is hotly contested. At huge environmental cost, it drives the spread of the consumerist lifestyle into millions of households. But since realization dawned that no amount of growth is going to extend the consumerist lifestyle to all – that the model demands social exclusion as its alter ego – the role of growth in a modified version of 'development' is much less clear-cut.

Patterns of growth

Different regions have fared very differently in terms of growth over recent decades. Some Asian countries, especially China and India, have seen spectacular growth. Others have decline in growth, or barely changed.

GDP per capita, average annual growth rates

	1970-90	1990-2010
Sub-Saharan Africa	0.0%	2.0%
South Asia	2.1%	4.5%
East Asia and Pacific	5.6%	7.4%
Latin America & Caribbean	1.4%	1.6%
Middle East & North Africa	−0.2%	2.4%
Industrialized countries	2.4%	1.6%
Least Developed Countries	−0.2%	2.6%

UNICEF, The State of the World's Children 2012

Economic progress is necessary for advances in social wellbeing, and there can be no release from poverty without economic growth. That at least remains a core development belief. And it is difficult to dispute. For one thing, there can be no spread of health and education services, roads and utilities, without the financial resources to pay for them. But then comes the question: how do you produce growth without an educated, healthy, connected, peaceful, physically secure, mobile and active population? So which comes first, the chicken or the egg?

Many now dispute the thesis that wealth has to be created before it can be redistributed, and insist that it has to be produced justly, redistributing as you go. Otherwise not only will a large number of people be left out altogether, but it may never be possible to produce the wealth at all. If large numbers of people descend into crime, violence, rage and destruction, growth will nosedive.

Leaving aside questions of resource exhaustion and planetary health, the question then becomes: how and where should this growth occur, and how much of it has to be invested in the social fabric both to maintain its own momentum and to avoid impoverishment and exclusion? Can it be generated without further eroding the fragile life-support systems of millions of families? If, as currently constructed, it actually excludes them from productive and dignified lives, then something has to change.

How did we get here?

In the early years of the mission, five-per-cent average increases in GNP were surpassed in many developing countries, thanks to robust prices for the minerals, oil and agricultural export crops around which colonizers had organized their satellite economies. The new wealth did not 'trickle down'; most developing-world govern-ments wanted cement factories, steel plants, roads, dams and airports. Redistribution would come later.

In the 1970s, the prices for their raw materials began to drop. After OPEC's successful hike of oil prices, the Group of 77 tried to negotiate better deals for other commodities in a 'New International Economic Order'. Despite early hopes, in the end nothing came of this. Prices for copper, tin, sugar, coffee and tea continued to decline. Non-oil-producing developing countries, especially the poorest, were hard hit. Between 1980 and 1991, they lost $290 billion due to lower prices for their exports, but they had to pay more for essential manufactured imports.[12]

The huge petrodollar windfall accruing to OPEC members ought surely to have been used for productive investment in impoverished neighbors. Here, finally, was the cash – $310 billion between 1972 and 1977 – for redistribution: investment on a massive scale that protagonists for an end to world poverty had sought since the 'big push' began. Instead, a travesty occurred – a travesty in which Western banks and key financial institutions on the one hand, and Southern dictators and governing elites on the other, colluded. Some of the OPEC wealth went on showpiece construction. But much of it wound up invested in equity markets or deposited in Western banks.

The banks were desperate to lend, and lend they did to loan-hungry Southern borrowers for a variety of loss-making ventures. Some went into the pockets of corrupt regimes and kleptocrats who, during the Cold War, were immune from economic scrutiny if their alliance was valued, and if they bought Western products, including arms. Some regimes in the Middle East entered their trajectory to fantastic wealth, since used for their own (economic and cultural) 'colonial' projects.

Not productivity but debt

As balance-of-payments crises multiplied and the debt burden on poor countries grew, the IMF and the World Bank imposed 'structural adjustment' in return for rescue packages. This prescription for economic health was steeped in the Thatcher-Reagan orthodoxies of deregulated markets, dismantling of trade barriers, privatization, the shrinkage of government, and cutbacks in social expenditures. In this economic world view, redistribution did not even feature. If the burden of bail-outs fell heaviest on those with least, that was too bad.

In a forerunner of today's 'age of austerity' in the industrialized world, 1980s structural adjustment in the South involved massive lay-offs in the public sector, spiralling unemployment, and cuts in budgets for health, education and social safety nets. Exports to earn foreign exchange were preferred to investment in basic necessities and domestic food production. Adjustment helped rescue international creditors from their bad loans and assisted the penetration of the South by transnational corporations, but it caused many already struggling economies to shrink.

So both debt and the measures imposed for its redemption served to push poor communities living in the cracks of the tottering modern economy into deeper trouble. As the national cake shrank or its product melted away in debt repayments, poor people's claim on a slice of it declined disproportionately. If services and livelihood incentives barely reached them in the past, now they were positively discriminated against. Their vulnerability became acute.

Thanks to the Jubilee 2000 crusade in the North, and to debt activists in the South, the pointlessness and injustice of forcing countries to cripple themselves further paying interest on criminally misguided loans began to have an effect. A series of debt-cancellation schemes were agreed, culminating in the Gleneagles G8 Summit in 2005. To date, $135 billion of debt has been cancelled for 35 low-income countries.[13]

Despite the illusory promise of the 2005 campaign to 'Make Poverty History', the poverty of the least well-off was never going to be ended by debt relief. Today, despite cancellations, the continuation of debt repayments means that more people move down to join them. In Jamaica, for example, 97 per cent of children completed primary school in 1990, while today the proportion is 73 per cent. For every 100,000 births in 1990, 59 mothers died, while today the number is 110. Africa today spends $21 billion a year on debt repayments, a figure that compares with the $30 billion it receives in aid.[14]

Now it is Europe's turn. The scourge of debt has now migrated from South to North and 'austerity packages' with many identical features have replaced structural adjustment. The creditors who cause the problems are protected, and the least responsible or able to cope pay the price.

Entering logo-land

Debt and deregulation – known misleadingly as liberalization – are companions at arms with the new behemoths of economic growth, the transnational corporations. In the last quarter of the 20th century, they became the principal designers and controllers of the economy in which those who could afford to ate, drank, smoked, dressed, drove, played sports, surfed the worldwide web and watched TV.

In 25 years the numbers of these corporations grew from 7,000 to 38,000, with 250,000 subsidiaries, spreading an identikit lifestyle all over the world.[15] Although half the world's population cannot afford to join in, that still leaves markets of hundreds of millions who can. These corporations and their offshoots now conduct two-thirds of the world's trade, and they decide worldwide where, what, how and for whom their output will be produced. Many are richer – and more powerful – than nation states. Their ascendance, in the phrase

Transnational behemoths

The profits of some transnational companies are larger than the GNI of a number of countries

Nestlé: $32.84bn ≥ GNI of 82 countries, including	Paraguay • Trinidad & Tobago • Luxembourg • Cambodia • Honduras • Albania • Botswana • Estonia • Cyprus • Macau SAR • Senegal • Macedonia • Georgia • Mozambique • Democratic Republic of Congo • Burkina Faso • Madagascar • Jamaica • Brunei • Gabon
Microsoft: $18.76bn ≥ GNI of 62 countries, including	Mauritius • Zambia • Armenia • Equatorial Guinea • Papua New Guinea • Nicaragua • Mali • Laos • Tajikistan • Namibia • Benin • Chad
Apple: $14.01bn ≥ GNI of 50 countries, including	Congo • Malawi • Rwanda • Moldova • Haiti • Kyrgyzstan • Niger • Malta • Guinea • Mongolia • Iceland • Bahamas • Montenegro • Mauritania • Swaziland • Togo • Barbados • Sierra Leone • Lesotho • East Timor • Suriname • Fiji • Bhutan • Central African Republic • Burundi • Eritrea • Guyana • Maldives • Gambia • Djibouti • Belize • Cape Verde • Seychelles • St Lucia • Antigua & Barbuda • Guinea-Bissau • Liberia • Solomon Is • St Vincent & The Grenadines • Vanuatu • Grenada • St Kitts & Nevis • Dominica • Comoros • Samoa • Tonga • Micronesia • Kiribati • São Tome & Principe • Palau

of Wolfgang Sachs, the growth model's most verbally elegant debunker, 'denationalized development'.[16]

The giant logo-land they promote is the familiar face o f globalization, and the part which has been most heralded as improving the economic prospects of the developing world by creating jobs and purchasing power. And although there are many appalled critics of the sweatshop conditions in which cloth es, electronic gadgets, toys, computer parts and a host of other products are made – often in 'export processing zones' where the companies enjoy freedom from taxes and labor regulations – it is hard to make out that they have done nothing at all for people in poor societies. The employment of women in the garment export industry of Bangladesh, for example, brought them a status they never enjoyed before.

What also cannot be denied, however, is that the power these companies exert is devoid of moral purpose: the top line and the bottom line are profit, not the advancement of the human condition. Poverty, in the form of rock-bottom wages, is the 'comparative advantage' these environments offer. If labor is cheaper and as malleable elsewhere, if better deals can be cut for tax holidays and the political environment is more secure, the women of Bangladesh will lose their jobs tomorrow. The 'free trade' treaties sponsored by the World Trade Organization (WTO) pave the way. So do compliant authorities keen to bring in investment.

Another side of the picture is the image of the good life peddled to the next generation of the global market's would-be consumers – that condemns them as second-class citizens. Fantasies of affluence, freedom and power flash via TV and pocket-sized screens into the remotest places, opening a window onto a fairytale world, but no door to get there. The global monoculture these images purvey destroys the values of ancient societies with shocking speed, its tentacles reaching into their existing way of life with crushing effect. Their familiarity with images of modern life comes with growing awareness of their exclusion. People whose way of life once had self-sufficiency and self-respect become insecure appendages to its embrace, reduced to menial and servile labor at its fringes.

The social anthropologist Helena Norberg-Hodge has written eloquently of the damage wrought by the introduction of money into the subsistence economy of Ladakh (in Kashmir, India). In the 1970s, the existing economy supported a high standard of living compared to that in most shantytowns. Before the arrival of an unstable monetary system, the Ladakhis were not 'poor' at all. Once they accepted meagre wages or grew crops for distant markets, they became dependent on forces beyond their control – transport, oil prices, international finance. 'Increasingly, people are locked into an economic system that pumps resources out of the periphery into the center. Often, these resources end up back where they came from as commercial products, packaged and processed, at prices the poor can no longer afford.'[10]

The world trade negotiations brokered by the WTO which began in 2001 and are known as the 'Doha Development Round' have repeatedly failed to reach agreement. Negotiators from developing countries who want to join the globalizing mainstream find the terms offered profoundly discriminatory. Northern commercial interests, masquerading as development proponents, only cut deals that suit themselves. Contrary to much anti-poverty rhetoric, a global trade package would make indigenous, organic forms of development in non-industrialized contexts an impossibility.

Neoliberal excess

Populist protest against globalization began in the late 1990s. In 2002, the Nobel laureate and ex-World Bank economist Joseph Stiglitz took up the cause of 'Globalization and its discontents'. Here was an authoritative voice explaining that international backing for a neoliberal one-size-fits-all economic agenda in countries without effective administrative institutions, functional laws, inclusive political or justice systems was bound to hurt the poor.[17]

In 2008, capitalism unbound, with all its financial deregulation trimmings, managed to all but crash the global economy. The huge hole that had to be plugged cost an incredible $30 trillion in damage.[18] Since then, the volume of authoritative analysis taking issue with market supremacy as an acceptable route to global prosperity has become a roar. In 2014, Mark Carney, Governor of the Bank of England, commented: 'Just as any revolution eats its children, unchecked market fundamentalism can devour the social capital essential for the long-term dynamism of capital itself.' But so far even severe criticism from within its own ranks has failed to consign the architects of neoliberal excess to history.

At the beginning of the development era, there were two available systems for economic organization: capitalist and communist. The triumph of the capitalist model with its energy-inducing dynamics – its ubiquitous drive for capital accumulation, and its co-option of technology and science in a ceaseless competition for market share – was famously declared to have brought about the 'end of history'. In spite of doing no such thing, and despite repeated calls for a new international social contract putting people first, an alternative to the relentless logic of neoliberal growth has yet to gain serious political ground.

So anxious and inward-looking has the industrialized world become about financial crisis, deficits, recession and unemployment closer to home that the predicament of the global disadvantaged has become eclipsed. The economic miracle of China and huge growth in countries such as India are seen as threatening, dramatically changing the sense of who needs help where. Surely their poor are *their* responsibility now? It can be hard to keep alive the old idea of the poorer half of humanity requiring beneficent inputs from the richer half, when 'their own' rich do not care.

Can small still be beautiful?

In the 1970s, an earlier phase of mass revulsion against the doctrine of unfettered growth and of belief that science and technology's pact with capital was positively Faustian, gave birth to a worldwide campaign for alternatives. Much of what this campaign produced is still extant, and its network of inheritors have added new ideas to a useful portfolio. The energy associated with many of these ideas still fuels worldwide social and environmental activism.

People then became aware for the first time that humanity was consuming the earth's supply of non-renewable resources at a self-destructive rate. Demographic trends – the population 'explosion' – meant that the speed of consumption was accelerating not only in the industrialized but in the developing world. The idea of 'Limits to growth' – the title of a landmark report – was powerful and chilling. If these limits were real, then the idea of development, both as means and end, had to change. We have been here before, but now the case is even more urgent.

Apart from introducing the concept of an ecological system and the need to preserve its integrity, this alternative thinking was – still is – revolutionary. The guru of 'small is beautiful', EF Schumacher, decried the chicanery of economics, with its celebration of 'the market' and 'economies of scale'. He deplored the 'idolatry of giantism', and suggested that any model of development which began from quantitative premises was bound to fail.

The solution he proposed was to start where people are, and build on their existing skills and managerial capacity. In semi-subsistence economies, intermediate forms of technology were needed, at far lower cost and on a much more sympathetic scale, to meet people's real requirements. From small beginnings – a vegetable plot or a tea-stall – someone might become the owner of a general store. Schumacher was accused of peddling development, second-class. But his ideas had huge resonance in civil society in both North and South.

The idea of development from the bottom up was echoed in the 'basic communities' of Brazil, by Tanzania's rural socialist experiment of *ujamaa*, and by community-based and people-led initiatives in India, Central America, and elsewhere. If development were authentically bottom-up, it would produce growth at the community level, but on such a small scale that unless it was replicated thousands of times over this would not be reflected in national Gross National Product (GNP). In this version of development, what mattered were the livelihoods of people and communities. The involvement and ownership of these processes by their 'beneficiaries', recast as actors with decision-making responsibilities, was integral to these ideas.

It took years for any of these approaches to be taken seriously by bureaucrats, politicians, or by the banking or commercial sector. When margins are tiny and everything takes time, where there is no prospect of large or speedy returns on investments, the curtain of invisibility is difficult to raise.

The advent of microcredit

Some kinds of 'small is beautiful' concepts managed eventually to break through into the mainstream. In 1976, when Bangladesh was undergoing famine, Mohamed Yunus, a professor of economics at Dhaka University, visited a village just outside the campus. He found that a woman making bamboo stools earned the daily equivalent of 2 cents' profit on an output of 22 cents. Her economy had no connection with the economics he taught, and he set out to remedy this state of affairs.[19]

His experiments led in 1983 to the creation of the Grameen Bank, an institution which upended all banking conventions to lend money in tiny amounts to the most economically excluded people in Bangladesh – landless women. Representing 96 per cent of Grameen's borrowers, these women had no collateral and were regarded as 'unbankable' from every point of view. Grameen's staff met potential clients in their homes, and peer groups of borrowers committed themselves to a lending and repayment code, and to adopt certain social habits: house improvement, vegetable growing, and sending children to school.

Except at periods of devastating natural disaster, the repayment rate was over 95 per cent. The millions of small lenders owned the bank, which secured employment for thousands of people. The model was so successful that it has since been exported to 58 other countries, including the US.

Yunus was not the only pioneer in micro-loan financing. Esther Ocloo of Ghana and Ela Bhatt of India – both working with market women in the informal economy – helped set up Women's World Banking in 1979. Like Yunus, they initially accepted soft loans from international bodies to recycle them in tiny amounts to customers; but the ultimate aim was self-sufficiency – dependence on people's own energy and resourcefulness. In the 40-odd years since these organizations led the way, others in countries such as the Philippines, Jordan, Bolivia and Zambia have followed suit. In 2010, the number of their clients in countries all over the world reached over 200 million, with around two-thirds consisting of the very poor.[20]

In 2006, Yunus shared a Nobel Prize with his creation, the Grameen Bank. An independent survey in 2009 showed that, between 1990 and 2008, 10 million Bangladeshis in receipt of loans surmounted the $1.25 poverty threshold.[21] Since then, the reputation of microfinance has suffered, with unscrupulous operators jumping on the bandwagon and NGO partnerships with international companies imploding.

In 2010, in the Indian state of Andhra Pradesh, a scandal emerged when aggressive loan-selling by unregulated micro-lending firms pushed large numbers of already desperately poor farmers into drastic levels of debt and even suicide.[22] Once profit is included in the model, microcredit is vulnerable to capture by private capital seeking high returns. If social purpose is lost, loan sharks, multiple interest and pressures to repay end up mimicking the moneylender behavior that Grameen set out to replace. In ways reminiscent of the subprime mortgage racket in the US and pay-day lending in the UK, money marketeers make mincemeat of the

How to help the poor: give them money

For decades, a cardinal development rule was: don't give the poor money. Spend whatever you must to reach the poor, educate the poor, enable the poor, empower the poor, but under no circumstances give them any cash – that would be a hand-out, not the hand-up that development is supposed to represent.

In the 1990s, a Brazilian program called Bolsa Familia broke this rule. It was a scheme like those in industrialized countries, where people routinely receive cash pensions and benefits as entitlements. Bolsa Familia was the centerpiece of President Lula's social policy. It gave people Conditional Cash Transfers (CCTs) as incentives to send children to school, have them vaccinated and so on: hence the 'conditionality'. Since then, CCT schemes have been replicated in the Americas, Asia and Africa. They vary in modality but are directed at those with low incomes, disabilities, those unable to work, the elderly and infirm, the war-widowed.

CCT schemes have defied the skeptics. The provision of money in hand on a regular basis to people who have very little access to the cash economy has been so effective that the schemes are now ubiquitous. Some are now less conditional and more like universal child benefit or a basic allowance.

The effects have often proved transformative. Family welfare improves; the situation of the most vulnerable improves; the household economy grows as many people start small enterprises; savings provide a cushion against shock; and people manage to get out of debt. The World Bank recently conducted a study showing that CCTs also help reduce child labor.

unprotected poor. The guardians of microfinance have fought back, with redesigned strategies and safeguards to defend their mission.[23]

Small-scale entrepreneurship fuelled by small-scale loans or other financing arrangements – the latest popular device is the Conditional Cash Transfer (CCT) – remain important alternative paths to economic advancement for the poor. As long as the system operates within the economy of the customers, and is equipped to take trouble with tiny loans and mini-transactions, micro-finance and the services surrounding it provide a genuine route out of poverty. The micro-finance and cash-transfer pioneers have shown that bridges can be built between traditional and modern economies. But they require sound management and determination to buck the deregulated, anti-benefit, state-shrinking, greed-enhancing tide.

Building more bridges

The expansion of the global marketplace cannot be dismissed as an unqualified evil, even if it has been accompanied by many acts of gross inhumanity. These not only include displacements, but disasters such as the collapse of the Rana Plaza factory – a 'temple of slave labor' – in Dhaka, Bangladesh. On 24 April 2013, 1,100 people, mostly women garment workers making clothes for international firms, lost their lives. But if all today's Rana Plazas were closed down, their workers would be destitute and other ramshackle factories would soon appear elsewhere.

For many of the workers employed by the global economy's contractors and subsidiaries, what must be looked for is not an end to their jobs but more security, better pay and improved working conditions. At the same time, it does not seem too much to ask that more attempts be made to build bridges – carefully, with genuine commitment to social responsibility – from existing invisible economies to modern outcrops. At present, too many local ways of life are being ground into dust or turned into a heritage museum marketed to tourists.

There are many development commentators in the South who echo Helena Norberg-Hodge's call for 'counter-development', a decentralized process that permits diversity, and builds on, rather than destroys, local systems. It has to be the case that there are other ways out of 'poverty' than for everyone to become card-carrying members of a high capital- and energy-intensive society – for which several more planetfuls of resources would anyway be required.

Unfortunately, few members of the development establishment seem able to think outside standard economic constructs. They do not make the effort to understand economies other than their own. They think grand investment on a massive scale is needed, when at community level millions of very tiny investments, carefully and collectively planned, would be far better. If the investors cannot operate at that level, then you would think they could manage to operate at one or two rungs up. But they rarely even try.

Those who show that there are alternatives are fêted and given platform-room at international meetings. Their critiques of what is happening in the name of development are vigorously applauded, but they do not lead to a revision of basic principles. Their ideas are appropriated but the lessons are only absorbed in a synthetic and peripheral way.

Somehow, if poverty-reduction goals and strategies are larded with the right vocabulary – 'resilience', 'equity', and 'sustainable' are current flavors of the day – the development professionals think that they have dealt with the biases, obstructionism and sheer lack of concern which disqualify so many groups of 'poor' from productive economic life. If more of them actually took the trouble to familiarize themselves with the realities of such people's lives, maybe they would be able to see how cosmetic much policy tinkering actually is. Then, perhaps, they might find ways to make useful links – useful from everyone's perspective – between multi-million-dollar investment packages and people whose resource base is vanishing from beneath their feet.

In the meantime, since economic growth, either pre- or post-globalization, failed to end poverty after all, it has been accepted that development has to have a social dimension. That is where we turn next.

1 Thomas Piketty, *Capital in the Twenty-First Century*, Belknap Harvard, 2014, pp 59-61 **2** *Human Development Report 1999*, UNDP/Oxford University Press. **3** Oxfam's 2014 Report *Even it up*, and subsequent report in January 2015, nin.tl/Oxfamoninequality **4** Brian Tomlinson, in *The reality of aid 2014*, Chapter 4, p 134, nin.tl/realityofaid **5** Suzanne Goldenberg, 'Aid packages ignore starving Afghans', *The Guardian*, 4 Feb 2002. **6** Deepa Narayan, with Raj Patel, Kai Schafft, Anne Rademacher, Sarah Koch-Schulte, *Can anyone hear us?* Book 1 of the Voices of the Poor study, Oxford University Press and World Bank, 2000. **7** Maggie Black, 'They only "hold pen"', *New Internationalist* 336, Jul 2001. **8** Sunil Khilnani, 'Difficult, yes; unjust often', essay on the play 'Beyond the beautiful forevers', National Theatre, Oct 2014. **9** Krishnan Guru-Murthy, 'India's dash for coal threatens ancient forests', *The Guardian*, 31 Oct 2014. **10** Nigam Prusty and Krishna N Das, 'India clears order to ease land acquisitions in reforms push', *Wall Street Journal* (Europe edition), 29 Dec 2014. **11** Suzanne Goldenberg, 'Dustbowls and hunger: environmental pioneer's valedictory warning', *The Guardian*, 25 Feb 2015. **12** Wayne Ellwood, *The No-Nonsense Guide to Globalization*, New Internationalist, 2010. **13** Nick Dearden, 'All together now!', *New Internationalist* 474, Jul/Aug 2013. **14** Global Justice Now, 'Dangerous Delusions', Myth 6, Jan 2015, nin.tl/daqngerousdelusions **15** Oswaldo de Rivero, *The Myth of Development*, Zed Books and others, 2001. **16** Wolfgang Sachs, 'Liberating the world from development', *New Internationalist* 460, March 2013. **17** Joseph Stiglitz, *Globalization and its discontents*, Penguin 2002. **18** Clifford Longley, 'Just money: How Catholic Social Teaching can Redeem Capitalism', Theos Report, London, 2014. **19** Mohamed Yunus with Alan Jolis, *Banker to the Poor*, Aurum Press, 1998. **20** 'Resilience: The State of the Microcredit Summit Campaign Report 2014', nin.tl/stateofcampaign **21** '10 million Bangladeshis Move above $1.25 a Day' grameen.com **22** Jason Burke, 'Impoverished Indian families caught in deadly spiral of microfinance debt', *The Guardian*, 31 Jan 2011, nin.tl/microfinancesuicides **23** The Microfinance Summit Campaign, State of the Campaign 2014 Report, microcreditsummit.org

4 Social progress matters

Although the economic players have occupied development's commanding heights, those engaged in social issues have dramatically increased their visibility and recognition over time. These components of the development puzzle gained their highest ascendancy in the Millennium Development Goals agenda, with its acknowledgement that any drive against poverty should focus at least as much on people's wellbeing as on national balance sheets. The policy priority may now be there, but what is the practical record?

When Robert McNamara, then its president, persuaded the World Bank in 1973 to redirect its policies towards the poorest 40 per cent of citizens in developing countries, a Rubicon was crossed. No longer was 'development' a purely economic concept, but it embraced social purpose too. Those laboring in the social vineyard were no longer seen merely as care providers or humanitarians offering first aid. They too were pursuing development and deserved some credibility.

It was not actually news to the social players – government, international and NGO – that they were contributing to the development process. Since the 1950s, the World Health Organization (WHO) and the UN Children's Fund (UNICEF) had supported mass onslaughts against disease throughout the developing world. This was the 'new look' in public health, made possible by advances in medical science such as vaccines and antibiotics. Malaria failed to succumb entirely to a worldwide mosquito killing spree but it was significantly reduced. The eradication of smallpox succeeded. The campaigns, heralded as prestigious success stories, had a remarkable effect in saving lives, especially in Asia, where their demographic impact was also quickest to raise concern.

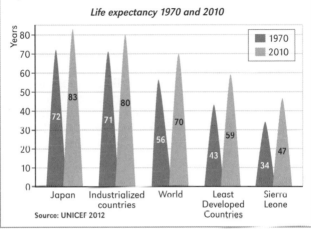

Social progress

The improvement of an average of 25% in life expectancy worldwide since 1970 is remarkable. But the gulf between the highest and lowest is still vast.

Life expectancy 1970 and 2010

Years

- ■ 1970
- ■ 2010

	Japan	Industrialized countries	World	Least Developed Countries	Sierra Leone
1970	72	71	56	43	34
2010	83	80	70	59	47

Source: UNICEF 2012

The disease campaigns were the main technical fix offered by the machinery of international public health, but not its only pursuit. The predominant motif of underdevelopment was the hungry child, and in the 1960s and 70s, malnutrition was a major concern. To begin with, the culprit was seen as insufficient protein. 'Protein malnutrition' was seen as an epidemic 'disease' in young children, to be tackled by a dietary medicine. So in the heyday of belief in technology's transcendent role, scientists set out to grind oilseeds, fish and peanuts and manufacture solutions to the 'protein crisis'. Eventually it transpired that protein was not the demon of malnutrition: calories were more important. However, no scientific fix can be found to deal with persistent hunger, even though the genetic modifiers – successors to the protein protagonists – today carry on as if they could.

Child nutrition again came to the fore when in 1981

the World Health Assembly passed an International Code to control the marketing of infant formula. The damage this had caused to infant health – formula made with unsafe water can be a death sentence for babies, and lacks the powerful health protective qualities of breastmilk – was a bellwether of what could happen when business corporations sought to penetrate their wares into societies that lacked the knowledge or means to use them properly. WHO and UNICEF also backed a support program for breastfeeding in hospitals and clinics to offset the companies' marketing claims. 'Baby-friendly' became a hugely successful movement. A World Alliance for Breastfeeding Action continues to

Child mortality

The global reduction in mortality in children under five years old is 60% since 1970. However, in sub-Saharan Africa, the numbers of deaths are actually higher (3.7 million in 2010 compared to 3.1 million), because of population increase.

Under-5 mortality (per 1,000 live births) by region, 1970 and 2010

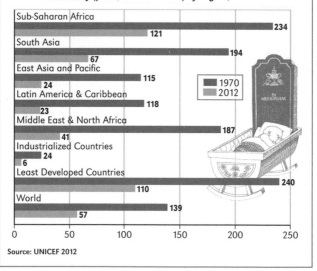

Sub-Saharan Africa: 234, 121
South Asia: 194, 67
East Asia and Pacific: 115, 24
Latin America & Caribbean: 118, 23
Middle East & North Africa: 187, 41
Industrialized Countries: 24, 6
Least Developed Countries: 240, 110
World: 139, 57

Legend: 1970, 2012

Source: UNICEF 2012

carry the banner forward and the International Baby Food Action Network continues to campaign against breaches of the Code.[1]

The appeal of the mass campaign for fixing health has never died. New campaigns have been conducted on behalf of 'essential drugs' and HIV treatments, as well as polio eradication. The Global Fund to fight AIDS, Tuberculosis and Malaria launched in 2002, with support from Bill Gates, and PEPFAR, the US President's Emergency Plan for AIDS Relief set up in 2008, have brought anti-retroviral drugs to millions of people living with HIV, even in remote African villages, and distributed 450 million insecticide-treated nets against malaria.[2] Considerable advances have been made in efforts to prevent and treat these epidemic diseases.

In nutrition, the story is different. Campaigns to end conditions caused by micronutrient deficiency – iron, Vitamin A, iodine – have moved ahead,[3] but the issue of undernutrition has languished. An inadequate diet, after all, is less the product of ignorance or specific nutrient deficiency than lack of a secure hold on the means to a livelihood. 'Entitlement' to a supply of food, as the Nobel Laureate economist Amartya Sen famously argued, is the point.[4] That is fundamentally a political issue, to be returned to in due course.

A patchy record

Addressing social as opposed to economic issues not only requires developing policies targeted towards the majority, thereby including the poor, but also requires delivering programs and services. Economists deal in policies, usually of the financial kind, but they do not normally design or deliver services. Policies, or anyway their principles, can be designed in an international space. But programs and services can only be delivered on the ground. A splendid policy for healthcare, child protection or adult literacy may be developed at international or national level, but without well-trained, adequately-staffed and properly resourced services to deliver it, nothing much changes.

Campaigns, especially those with a technical fix to offer such as inoculations or condoms, are relatively straightforward: many components are standard, mass produced in controlled circumstances, and their distribution and administration can be centrally planned and – with good logistics – 'rolled out'. But the building up of knowledge and practice in soil management, environmental health, childhood care and other areas key to lasting social change cannot be done in campaign fashion. The transformation of attitudes and behaviors takes time. No master plan for three days of immunizations or ten days of village drain construction will do the trick. Building self-sufficiency among the poor, at their pace and within their managerial capacity, is difficult, as all program people will attest. Still, a misplaced belief remains among development's high priesthood that such things can be ordained and orchestrated from the policy center.

The context of program delivery, not the policy, is the hard part, however carefully the policy designers try to take all the difficulties – via 'bottleneck analysis' and other new development disciplines – into account. Run the gamut of activity in the social sectors over time and you will find far more failures relating to program context than policy principle, courtesy of factors at ground level that no-one took into account. The weather, for example: extremely high or low temperatures may be ignored, so that a building – a toilet, or a classroom – is unusable. Or density of settlement: where houses are close together and living-space confined, the uptake of sanitation will be totally different from where homes are very spread out. Cultural attitudes can make or break. Where maximization of family size is the norm, few people will welcome family planning. Ways of doing things that have served people well for generations are not instantly abandoned because newcomers extol the virtues of things for which there is no existing sense of need, and promote weird ideas such as confining ordure in smelly latrines or keeping grown-up girls in school.

The governmental record in the social sphere has been patchy, not surprisingly. In rural areas of most of the developing world – and in poor urban areas as these multiply – the service network remains embryonic. At the beginning of the development era, existing health, schooling or welfare services in many parts of the poor world were provided by saints, missionaries or humanitarian entrepreneurs in small, scattered oases for a surrounding clientele. The development of functional countrywide government networks was a daunting proposition, especially on paper-thin budgets. Decades later, it remains a major challenge. The latest global orthodoxy of cutting state service provision in the name of reducing deficits and dependency and encouraging 'resilience' is not going to help. Today's saints, missionaries and humanitarian entrepreneurs will be left carrying the burden.

The problem with 'scaling up'

When the big-league players began to intervene in the social sphere, their original idea was that the various sectoral activities should be 'integrated'. Roads, clinics, water supplies, transport, communications, schools, would be introduced in tandem in a given area. The problem with these plans was that integration rarely extended beyond them. Meetings might take place at the center, but out in 'the field' synchronized inputs for socio-economic transformation were an illusion. People would arrive one day and build something; different people would arrive some months later and build something else. This happened without reference to the views of local people and whether they wanted these installations.

Another model was the 'pilot project'. A prototype for provision of village water supplies or women's income-generating groups would be tried out in a particular setting, and when its bugs had been ironed out it would be 'replicated' or 'scaled-up' district-wide. Sometimes this was expected to happen spontaneously: people in nearby communities would see the value of the new standpipes and envy the women their new skills, and demand would spread.

Unfortunately, 'scaling up' often proved a delusion too. The bugs were never ironed out, or the benefits not as compelling as expected. Some things – child protection for example – cannot be 'scaled up' like a vaccination campaign; each new iteration has to be started afresh. Yet today, the idea of 'scaling up' is still repeated like a mantra, as if like a twitter feed, social improvement can be made to trend. People who should know better are still advocating silver bullets and golden keys.

Jeffrey Sachs' Millennium Villages Project, with major backing from George Soros, injected $120 million over 10 years, into 14 African villages containing 500,000 people. Sachs' 'integrated and replicable' model aimed to speed up social and economic development at the grassroots by a strategic mix of 'scalable' inputs.[5] No-one can resist the quest for short cuts, but they don't exist. Only after the big money stops rolling in does it become clear whether changes are lasting. Without continued inputs, they usually aren't. Sachs' much-criticized Millennium Villages have only managed to prove an old lesson: never mind what sum is available, there is no alternative to moving at the pace of any given community, with their leaders, doing things that match their priorities. Development has to be their show, not ours.[6]

NGOs tend to be much more realistic. Partly because they are bit-players in financial terms for whom 'small' is the only option, they mostly engage in improving the condition of groups of people in seriously needy situations. They do not design mass programs at many stages removed from their target localities, and their reality checks are more effective. Almost all the radical thinking about how development might work for poor people has come from the social NGO players and most of it has been pioneered by local people – including incomers and some expatriates well-versed in local realities – with small amounts of external support.

Alternative models and 'barefoot' approaches

If the export of Western models failed to benefit poor people economically, the same held true in the social sphere. Where 90 per cent of a country's health budget was spent on a handful of high-tech hospitals dispensing medical care for the few, the health of 90 per cent of the country's population was ignored.

Many examples of alternative models for health services came to prominence in the 1970s. China's 'barefoot doctors', for example, who treated symptoms of common diseases, provided health education and referred cases they could not manage to those who could. A number of successful experiments were also undertaken by dedicated professionals in Bangladesh, Tanzania, Guatemala and elsewhere along similar decentralized lines. Their cumulated experience became the basis for WHO's adoption of a strategy for 'primary health care' whereby village-based workers would help communities achieve 'health for all'. At the heart of this model was public health advance: mother and child health services including safe childbirth, disease control and prevention, and education for health self-protection.

The ideology of those people-centric days was, at its extreme, very radical: some saw the democratization and demedicalization of healthcare as ends in themselves. Certainly, they represented a commitment to supporting people's own abilities to define and meet their needs. Today, many of those concerned with health policy regard WHO as having backtracked on its commitment to the poor. It has been co-opted by Big Pharma, and dropped its emphasis on the expansion of primary-healthcare systems. Grand-slam approaches and disease campaigns are back in fashion. Médecins sans Frontières has become a more effective protagonist than WHO of 'health for all', as its more committed and effective response to the 2014 West Africa ebola crisis demonstrated.

Education had to undergo a similarly radical overhaul. Not only was there a huge appetite for learning all over the developing world, but even the leading advocates of economic growth as the *sine qua non* of social improvement recognize that the nation-building project is impossible without educational expansion. But should the major investment be in primary education for the masses, or secondary and tertiary education for a tiny elite? In the late decades of the 20th century, education also experienced its radical phase, with 'barefoot' teachers, reintroduction of local languages as the medium of instruction, non-formal programs for women who had never gone to school and children who had 'dropped out'. Increased productivity and family wellbeing required that everyone – especially women – had a basic educational grounding: even the World Bank agreed with that.

These ideas, informed by a range of experiences in the South, came together in the 'basic services strategy'. This envisaged the extension of basic healthcare, water supply, sanitation, nutrition services to untouched communities through the agency of community-based workers. The services would have to respond to the real needs and desires of communities since they would run them. The authorities would supervise, co-ordinate, provide technical back-up and adjust inputs appropriately.

The promise of the 'basic services strategy' was higher than its yield: many developing-country governments resisted radically restructuring services towards their more deprived populations. Nonetheless, the impulse to design services so as to reach far-flung communities did have a lasting effect. So did the realization that people in 'poor' societies could be agents of change in their own lives and were not merely passive victims of hunger, ill-health and other characteristics of 'poverty'.

A new focus on software

The upending of standard models for social advance provided a laboratory from which emerged a new set of development tenets: 'participatory', 'decentralized', 'empowering', 'knowledge transfer' and 'community owned'. This was the 'how' – the software ingredients which knocked from their pedestal the all-powerful hardware ingredients and their overlords – engineers, planners and accountants. The emphasis on process was a corrective to the old idea that development was all about buildings, installations and technological devices. But it also helped introduce a degree of incoherence. If what was needed were year-round water supplies and schools with teachers, books and classrooms, 'knowledge transfers' and 'attitudinal change' were not enough. Tangible benefits were also needed.

As the focus of attention shifted to the community, the diversity of 'the poor' became more visible: poverty was not a uniform phenomenon and its victims could not all be lumped into one conceptual basket. The predicaments of women were increasingly recognized; children also become better noticed as a sub-group affected by social disintegration and family breakdown; and the need to promote human rights to survival, health, education and protection from exploitation and violence became a new development theme.

The attention to the software of development led to a greater emphasis on education. Study after study showed that every form of social and economic improvement depended on the amount and quality of education people, especially women, received. In the 1990s a global initiative for 'Education for All' was launched. This proposed universal access to a basic package of knowledge and skills, via universal primary education and non-formal 'catch-up' programs for adults.

At the same time the frustration felt by many social-development organizations at the slow pace of change began to express itself in another form of software:

'advocacy'. Organizations commissioned research, analyzed data and began to issue reports calling for policy change in every imaginable area. This generated prescriptions by the score and contributed to 'the policy debate'. At ground level, it also helped spread information and exert pressure on service providers. The outreach of mobile phones even to remote communities has since opened up many more communications and advocacy channels.

Links with economic concerns

A feature of social programs was that they quickly began to embrace economic and livelihood issues. Take women as an example. They used to be seen as home-makers with no economic significance. But they are key providers to the household as food producers and petty traders as well as supplying essential domestic care and nurturing services. Without recognition of their role in the household economy and family wellbeing, there could be few social impacts from raised productivity.

The new emphasis on women's role in development exposed the ways in which development had promoted gender discrimination, opening up educational and employment opportunity to men, and leaving women stranded in menial roles – a phenomenon known as 'the feminization of poverty'. In much of Africa, over three-quarters of rural women work constantly, in the fields or selling produce in the market; two-thirds do so in Southern Asia. While they constitute 30 per cent or less of the employed workforce, in the informal workplace they predominate: 84 per cent of African women working outside agriculture are in waste-collecting, brick-carrying, domestic work and similar unregistered and low-paid work; in Latin America, the proportion is 58 per cent.[7]

The women represented in these statistics work not as an act of liberated choice, but because they desperately need some cash. Women also provide social care and

A program originally designed to offer social benefits – better health, for example – may end up realizing benefits that are primarily economic.

Rajendra Singh, who trained as a health practitioner, originally went to Alwar district in the parched Indian state of Rajasthan in the mid-1980s to set up clinics. But villagers, faced with wells drying up, crops wilting and their menfolk leaving for town in droves, asked him instead for water.

At the suggestion of a village elder, Singh resurrected a traditional water-harvesting technology fallen into disuse. He built *johads* – small earthen embankments or 'check-dams' – in the beds of seasonal rivers to arrest rainwater during the monsoon.

Since then, the organization he formed, Tarun Bharat Sangh (TBS), has helped build 8,600 small dams and other rainwater harvesting structures. This has led to the regeneration of dried-up rivers and transformed the agricultural economy of over 1,000 villages. Two-thirds of structures were built without the help of an engineer, and at a ridiculously low cost compared to the concrete massifs favored by the planners.

The water table has risen from a depth of 61 to 9 meters, and after successive years of drought, most *johads* contain water when everything else is dry. Management is in the hands of local communities, who operate strict rules about water use, crops and tree-planting. Forest cover has increased and wild animals have returned.

Here is a classic example of starting where people are at and with their co-operation, using an existing technology, suitably modernized, to regenerate their own economy and its environmental base. Rajendra Singh has faced much governmental obstruction, but also gained recognition, most recently the prestigious 2015 Stockholm Water Prize.

healthcare, in their family roles and in the community. Because women fought for it, attention to gender roles and affirmative action to improve women's status have become a norm in development policy, even if real-life practice continues to be disappointing.[8]

In other social programs, economic components keep creeping in. There may be a need for maintenance of community installations or stipends for community workers. Few efforts to extend services entirely by government, even where it is willing, work well; facilities often break down or remain unused. Where communities pay for basic repair materials, services are better grounded, better 'owned' and used. Thus many social schemes rely on local systems of community levy, 'revolving funds', and subsidized sale of spare parts to get them fully established.

If the economics work, and the social improvement fits consumer reality – contracts with schools in western Kenya for vegetable provision, toilets in rural West Bengal and urban Senegal – it enters their own economy and generates its own mini-industry and local jobs. This is the antithesis of large-scale, across-the-board investments which are supposed to bring about total poverty 'lift-off' in a small span of years. In a more practical, modest way, social-development actors have found ways to build bridges between traditional economies and semi-formal and wider markets.

Demand and willingness to pay

The downside of the social actors' success in the livelihood context is that the economists have latched on to 'willingness to pay' as an indication of market demand's supremacy even in the social sphere, even among people with very few cash resources. They talk of 'full cost recovery' and advocate cuts in subsidies at the earliest opportunity, even when it is clear that many services cannot reach the unserved without subsidies, nor did they do so in the industrialized world.

In many Southern settings, the provision of services is already skewed by the realities of social hierarchy, wealth and political influence. They are subsidized in favor of the elite; it seems grossly unjust therefore to make people who are much worse off pay fully for them. Yet this is a cornerstone of the World Bank's poverty-reduction strategies – its latest display of commitment to the idea that social investments matter. Yes, they matter, but they will have to be paid for. This applies to healthcare, schooling, water and sanitation. In many African cities, even a bucket of water from a standpipe carries user-charges. People's 'willingness to pay' for things they cannot do without has been interpreted as an indication of their 'demand' – and become a stick with which to beat them.

Meanwhile, if there is evidence of a demand for services within a traditional economic framework, they will be commercialized by market advocates. People in informal occupations are cut out – water sellers, waste collectors, snack-food makers, for example. The prices of the new goods and services are invariably higher than those of the traditional providers they displace. 'Efficiency' requires involvement from the modern economy with its superior technology and know-how; but the higher costs of its apparatus and profits have to be passed down. Not only are services provided by commercial water and fuel companies unaffordable for those in low-income groups but they destroy the invisible economies on which informal systems were based. And so the carousel of exclusion goes around.

Social improvement – or destruction?

Some critics blame the social improvers almost as vehemently as the economic planners for the destruction of traditional lifestyles brought about by 'progress'. But many of the cultural practices they try to erode – female genital mutilation (FGM) and forced early marriage, for example – are indefensible, and opposed by many in the societies concerned. As the HIV and ebola epidemics underline, many beliefs surrounding the routes of infectious diseases need displacement by scientific fact.

It is also the case that the iniquitous intrusion of consumerism and modern technology into societies ill-prepared to apply them can make them more pernicious. For example, FGM carried out in hospital circumstances with anesthetic can mean that more of the genital area is cut away. The availability of cheap ultrasound tests to determine the sex of an unborn child is responsible for the widespread abortion of girls. In India, it is seen as the main contributor to the decline in the sex ratio between 1961 and 2011, from 975 to 914 females per 1,000 males.[9] Although its use for sex pre-selection is illegal, the practice is too lucrative for unscrupulous medical practitioners to abandon.

Sensitive social-development practitioners ease the transition from old ways to new and help people and communities make informed choices about the future. Other social activists hold the line against the forces of displacement. Today, those committed to social advance often have to spend their time seeking justice or compensation for the misery inflicted on the already disadvantaged by purveyors of developmental exclusion. This is not a romantic preoccupation with the past, but a confrontation over first principles which is becoming uglier by the day.

'Human' development at center-stage

In 1990, the UN Development Programme (UNDP) published the first of its annual Human Development Reports. This was an initiative of Mahbub ul Haq, previously a finance minister in Pakistan, who persuaded UNDP to give his project house room and a budget. The report opened as follows: 'The real wealth of a nation is its people. And the purpose of development is to create an enabling environment for people to enjoy long, healthy and creative lives. This simple but powerful truth is too often forgotten in the pursuit of material and financial wealth.'

Although social factors had been acknowledged as integral to development back in the 1970s, progress continued to be measured by the same economic criteria: growth in GNP per capita, which divides the national cake by the number of citizens, indicating nothing about their state of wellbeing. (Today, gross national income – GNI – per capita is the measure, but the same caveat applies.)

The Human Development Index (HDI)

The Human Development Index (HDI) was introduced in 1990 in the first Human Development Report. To show countries' performance by a measure less crude than per capita GDP, two social indicators – life expectancy and educational achievement – were added to income in a composite index. Since then, it has been widely accepted that development is not defined purely by economic output and has to reflect other indicators. At the same time HD methodology has been considerably refined. The position of a country on the HDI no longer has the impact it did when the Index was introduced. Better-off countries are invariably in the higher categories. But there are discrepancies which can be instructive about a country's emphasis on social capital building and equity. Note, for example, that Costa Rica is one-quarter as wealthy as Saudi Arabia, but not a lot lower in human development terms.

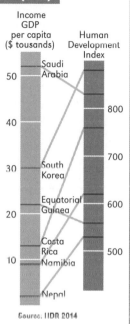

Source: HDR 2014

Haq was concerned that debt and structural adjustment were sending social indicators into reverse, and had long believed that a rethink about the underlying purpose of development was required. His emphasis on 'human development' helped start a process whereby improvements in social indicators such as child mortality, life expectancy, illiteracy and malnutrition became recognized internationally as defining characteristics of development instead of merely as adjuncts.

According to the 'Human Development Index' the Report proposed, a country – Sri Lanka or Cuba for example – might be poor according to standard economic criteria, but because it had made investments in education, health and 'social capital', had rates of literacy and life expectancy which raised its status closer to 'developed'. The idea was to prompt countries with reasonable incomes but weak social performance to reorient policies and resources so that economic success could be transformed into human wellbeing.

The ranking of countries against the index caused controversy, especially among those countries that performed poorly. But the idea helped build momentum against the centrality of GNP per capita as the gauge of development and redefined the terms of the debate. Although in later reports the leading exponents of 'human development' have sometimes seemed over-keen on refining their measuring tools, developing new indices for gender equality and other sub-sets of human development as an academic discourse, the lens has helped to change perspectives. No development expert today would describe global poverty without emphasizing such human manifestations as hunger and disease. In fact, there are instances today where 'development' is listed in a social bracket such as health, instead of under 'economics'.[10] Whether this will turn out to be a significant reconfiguration is as yet impossible to say.

MDGs and beyond

The first development organization chief to attempt to build a global alliance around time-bound social goals was UNICEF's Executive Director, James P Grant. He elevated the reduction of infant mortality to pole position in UNICEF's mission, and set out to generate political momentum behind 'child survival'. Grant resuscitated the disease campaign approach which had been eclipsed by 'basic services' and launched a drive for universal childhood immunization. Many countries' immunization rates soared, and Grant's big push for better vaccination technology and spread still carries momentum today.

The next step was the articulation of a number of global social goals, and their acceptance at a World

Summit for Children in 1990. These included reductions by 2000 in infant and young child mortality; maternal mortality, child malnutrition and illiteracy; universal access to safe water and sanitation and to primary education. In a number of countries, national programs of action were developed.

Ten years later, commitment to this new version of the development mission came to further fruition after the UN Millennium Summit. A set of goals was confirmed by the international community as the Millennium Development Goals with deadlines of 2015. A socially oriented push against poverty was launched, in which a worldwide constituency of international and national organizations was involved. The development mission thus received a long-overdue facelift to ensure that the human improvement it was always intended to secure would not be left to happen coincidentally as a product of economic advance.

A year before the final MDG count was due, the UN's annual report on progress recorded major advances. In several contexts there were some marked improvements over the period. The likelihood of a child dying before age five has been nearly halved in 20 years. The proportion

The MDGs – for achievement by 2015; baseline, 1990

- Reduce by 50 per cent the share of the world's people living on less than $1 a day and suffering from hunger
- Achieve universal primary education for all boys and girls
- Eliminate gender disparity in primary and secondary education
- Reduce mortality rates for children under five by 66 per cent
- Reduce maternal mortality by 75 per cent
- Halt, then reverse, the spread of HIV/AIDS, malaria and other major diseases
- Ensure environmental sustainability and reduce by half the proportion of people without access to safe drinking water
- Develop a global partnership for development committed to good governance and poverty reduction

un.org/millenniumgoals

Social progress matters

HIV: Signs of hope

The epicenter of HIV infection and suffering remains sub-Saharan Africa. But the rate of new infections is declining everywhere. So is the death rate, as access to antiretroviral treatment (ART) rises. At the end of 2013, 35 million people worldwide were living with HIV, of whom 12.9 million were receiving ART. If progress in controlling HIV spread and treatment take-up can be accelerated, the epidemic could be ended by 2030.

People living with HIV by country, 2013

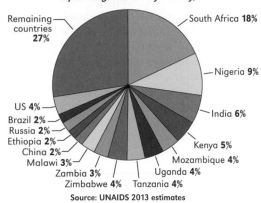

Source: UNAIDS 2013 estimates

HIV death rate trends in Africa

Globally, 15 countries account for nearly 75% of people living with HIV.

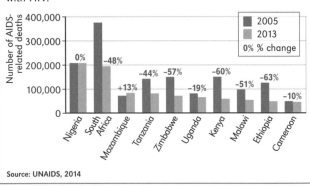

Source: UNAIDS, 2014

International Development

of people without access to safe drinking water has also been halved. Universal primary education may not be achieved, but 90 per cent of children in developing regions now go to school and gender disparities are lower. Maternal mortality is down by nearly half, and there have been major advances in the fight against malaria, tuberculosis and HIV.

Inevitably, the report is bound to adopt a 'cup half-full' rather than 'half-empty' approach. Some of the progress, especially in the life-expectancy and disease-control context, is real and unquestionable. However, using 1990 as the MDG baseline instead of 2000 gave a handy statistical boost, especially given the progress made by China in the 1990s. Computing numbers globally or by region disguises the lack of progress in some countries, especially the poorest, especially in Africa. And then there is the problem that, thanks to population growth, numbers as distinct from proportions have not necessarily dropped. If numbers only are examined and China is removed from the equation, the global poverty head count is the same today as in 1981.[11] The proportion of undernourished people has decreased from 24 per cent to 14 per cent since 1990, but most of this occurred in the 1990s and the numbers of the chronically hungry remain well above 800 million.[12]

Although several of the MDGs will not be met, there is no doubting the success of the agenda in keeping a humanity-centered version of development in the limelight and galvanizing resources from the new galaxy of superstar philanthropists. Now the international emphasis is on how to enhance the agenda after 2015. Accordingly, a broader and more ambitious set of Sustainable Development Goals (SDGs) for the 15 years until 2030 is being debated, and will be put to the UN late in 2015.

Goals reign supreme

The supremacy of the Goals agenda and the effort to

make it succeed have been a driving force. But there are some less positive aspects. The agenda is centrally set, it seems to be ballooning out of control with too many goals and targets for 2015-2030, some with a fuzziness that will make them impossible either to monitor or attain.[13]

The agenda gives off an echo of the old delusion that aid is instrumental in development, and that if only 'the Goals' can be met, the development mission will be accomplished. The community as the key locus of activity has been downgraded and the stress on measurability crowds out much that is important. This includes widening disparities in access to income and benefits, and to the vital need for participation of those the agenda is supposed to serve.

For many reasons – and they include failures of commitment on every side – the extension of universal affordable basic services is not going forward with anything like the momentum needed. Nor are livelihood schemes to assure people a basic 'entitlement': the means either to grow or to buy enough food for their families and to meet other essentials. Despite all the rhetoric about targeted poverty reduction, a quarter of the children in the developing world remain undernourished.

Somehow it has been forgotten that the people targeted by Goals ought to be democratically involved in deciding what needs to be done on their behalf and that, without their engagement, no progress is possible. If there was one thing the early mistakes of the development era established, it was the need for 'bottom-up' rather than 'top-down'. A generation later it all needs learning again.

Meanwhile, social stress continues to rise. Conflict, displacement, families decimated by crisis of one kind or another; those dependent on a sole woman earner; landless families, urban poor families; families with working children, children on their own. These constitute the 10 or 20 per cent, sometimes 50 per cent, of those whom services do not reach or who cannot afford to use them. Despite the major social gains in global terms, the proportions of those unreached remain high. Without radical policy change their outlook cannot improve.

1 See the Baby-friendly Hospital Initiative and WABA waba.org.my; IBFAN is at ibfan.org **2** Global Fund Results factsheet December 2014, theglobalfund.org/en/about/diseases See too pepfar.gov/about/index.htm **3** See The Micronutrient Report nin.tl/micronutrientreport **4** *Poverty and famines: An essay on entitlement and deprivation*, Amartya Sen, Clarendon Press, 1984. **5** Madeleine Bunting, 'Millennium Villages Project. does the "big bang" approach work?', *The Guardian*, 10 Oct 2011, nin.tl/villagequestions **6** See for example nin.tl/munkscritique **7** The World's Women 2010: Trends and Statistics, United Nations, nin.tl/worldswomen **8** *Gender Equality: Striving for Justice in an Unequal World*, UNRISD, 2005. **9** 'India's unwanted girls', BBC News South Asia, 23 May 2011, bbc.co.uk/news/world-south-asia-13264301 **10** See, for example, project-syndicate.org – a source of articles by a range of eminent writers in a range of areas, funded by the Bill and Melinda Gates Foundation. **11** Jason Hickel, 'The death of international development', *Red Pepper*, Feb 2015. **12** The Millennium Development Goals Report 2014, nin.tl/MDGprogress2014 **13** Jan Vandemoortele, 'Post-2015 agenda: mission impossible?' *Development Studies Research*, 2014, nin.tl/Vandemoortele

5 Enter 'sustainability'

The concept of 'sustainable development' reconciles the goal of economic progress with the need for environmental constraint. Three 'Earth Summits' have discussed with increasing urgency the destructive effect on planetary health of current development behavior. Today 'sustainable' is so well-established a soubriquet that it will even be used for the successors to the Millennium Development Goals. Could 'development' be redesigned to meet current threats to the global commons of climate, water, fuel and biodiversity, or does the idea contain an inherent contradiction?

In 1983, the UN Secretary-General invited Norwegian prime minister Gro Harlem Brundtland to chair a World Commission on Environment and Development. Concern about the pressure of population growth, modern technology and consumer demand on the planetary fabric had been smoldering away for some time. Now a new generation of environmental worries – global warming, deforestation, species loss, toxic wastes – had come to scientific and popular attention. The world's natural resources were being rapidly depleted, often in the name of development; but the poverty this was supposed to correct remained as widespread as ever.

Ever since environmental issues first appeared on the international agenda, a few voices linked the plunder of natural resources with world poverty.[1] But more attention was captured by dire prognostications of planetary disaster. Two of the most influential reports were *Limits to Growth* by the Club of Rome and *Blueprint for Survival* by the UK journal *The Ecologist*, both published in 1972. These alarm calls about rapid resource exhaustion sent shockwaves around the world. Their computer-modelled rates of energy depletion turned out to be exaggerated, but they exerted a powerful force on the human conscience and launched a new international crusade.

The problem with these early analyses of environmental stress was that they were biased against poor countries and especially against poor people within them. Their extraordinary fertility was blamed for precipitating a global population crisis. Plummeting death rates – for which the disease campaigns were responsible – had yet to be accompanied by declines in birth rates. In Asia and Africa, population growth rates had reached over two per cent a year.[2] The long-term implications were startling. World population had taken 120 years to grow from one to two billion, but just 35 years to reach three billion in around 1960. The speed of

World population increase

The bulk of world population increase has occurred very recently. The rate masks great variations between regions. In general, industrialized country populations are growing very little. Some countries, notably in the former Eastern bloc, have shrinking populations. 95 per cent of the increase in 2000 was in countries of the South.

World population: 1950-2050

World population growth rates: 1950-2050

Source: U.S. Census Bureau, International Data Base, June 2011 Update

growth was accelerating dramatically. In the subsequent 55 years, four more billions have been added at an average interval of less than 14 years.

The initial reaction was a Malthusian panic. How would a planet bursting at the seams manage to feed, shelter and provide for all these people? Doomsters predicted that, without a drastic curtailment of fertility, the development process could never accelerate fast enough to keep pace. Within a few generations, socio-economic progress would all have been devoured by its own children.

The 'population crisis'

India and China, the most populous countries, took this constraint very seriously. There was no time to wait for the 'demographic transition' – the drop in family size that accompanies a higher standard of living; in the industrialized world this had taken at least a generation. India introduced a draconian measure of enforced sterilization, but had to withdraw it in the face of social and political upheaval. China imposed its one-child policy in 1979.

Elsewhere, the call for fertility control fell mainly on deaf ears. Catholic countries – Latin America, the Philippines – were opposed. In Africa, larger populations were actively desired. Among small farmers in semi-subsistence economies, 'family planning' consisted of having large numbers of children since they were needed to provide labor and security in old age.

'Population control' became an anathema. Unwelcome attempts to browbeat people all over the developing world into swallowing pills and installing loops created a backlash. Having earned a bad name, the mass campaign model for family planning was dropped and the programs were absorbed into Maternal and Child Health (MCH) services. A different route to fertility reduction was proposed: female education plus better opportunities for women.

With rising incomes and increased urbanization,

the 'demographic transition' soon began in earnest and the global growth rate started to slow down. By 2012, it had declined to 1.1 per cent, and is expected to dwindle further. Although it will still take some decades before replacement only is reached, that prospect is now foreseeable. However, in the poorest groups in the poorest countries, fertility remains very high for the same reasons: family labor and old age support.

It is inescapable that population growth exerts huge pressures on the natural resource base and contributes to displacement: people pushed off the land to make way for expanding suburbs, plantations or mines. Migration and unplanned growth in the stretched urban fabric of the South leads to sprawling slums, pollution, human and environmental degradation. Fifty-four per cent of the world's population are now urban dwellers, and in developing regions the majority live in slums and shanties.[3]

This acute, poverty-driven, family-fragmenting population growth crisis in town and cities, with its associated crime and violence, has not yet captured the attention it deserves. Meanwhile, voices are once again sounding grim predictions about what will happen when there are nine or ten billion people on earth,[4] but they do not cause the stir they used to.

Planetary threats

The reason is simple. The 'population explosion' is not the major threat to the harmony of the planet. Almost all population growth is among poorer people. And they are not the ones consuming the earth's supply of fossil fuels, warming the globe with their carbon emissions, poisoning soil and water with their chemicals, or wreaking ecological havoc with their pollution. Their consumption of resources is minute compared to that of the industrialized world.

The Brundtland Report turned existing wisdom on its head, showing that poverty in the developing world is less cause than effect of environmental degradation, too often the outcome of insensitive technology transfer that pauperized people and natural systems. Threats to planetary health came from the lifestyles of the better-off, and the aspirations for a high-energy life – not only fuel, but extra water, and different kinds of food – that the promise of 'development' held out to millions of people in the South. Today, the same case in more urgent terms is made by Naomi Klein, who marks the year after Brundtland – 1988 – as a landmark one in which talks began about serious cuts in greenhouse-gas emissions, while the North American Free Trade Agreement (NAFTA) kicked off the era of globalization.[5]

If all the world's people were to live like North Americans, a planet four times as large would be needed. Thus, economic progress and the fulfilment of human needs has to be counterbalanced by the

The resource use gap

The chart shows the annual impact of 1,000 people i.n a developed and a developing country.

	In Germany		In a developing country	
158		Energy consumption (TJ)	22	(Egypt)
13,700		Greenhouse gases (t)	1,300	(Egypt)
450		Ozone depleting substances (kg)	16	(Philippines)
8		Roads (km)	0.7	(Egypt)
	4,391,000	Freight transports (tkm)	776,000	(Egypt)
	9,126,000	Passenger travel (pkm)	904,000	(Egypt)
443		Cars	6	(Philippines)
28		Aluminum consumption (t)	2	(Argentina)
	413	Cement consumption (t)	56	(Philippines)
655		Steel consumption (t)	5	(Philippines)
	400	Solid waste (t)	ca.120	(Philippines)
187		Hazardous waste (t)	ca. 2	(Philippines)

TJ = Tera Joule (1x1012 joules)   t = tons
tkm = ton kilometers   pkm = passenger kilometers

protection of air, soil, water and all forms of life – from which, ultimately, planetary stability is inseparable. It is not possible to continue with 'business as usual' and assure every person a healthy and productive life without jeopardizing the right of coming generations to their own slice of the world's pie. Thus the 'sustainable development' concept brought environmentalism into poverty reduction in a neat and simple formula.

In 1992 came the first Earth Summit. After this, the word 'sustainable' was absorbed into the development lexicon and has since been used to mean anything from 'environmentally sensitive' to 'respect for indigenous ways of doing things' to 'affordable over the longer term'.

So what has been the subsequent experience? Is sustainable development practicable, and if so, can it help the poor?

Overconsumption in the North

The idea of 'limits to growth' has from its inception provoked resentment from the developing world: a regime of international ecological regulation – not in place during Western industrialization – would, they claimed, deny them a 'developed' future. Blocks on resource use would fix the world in permanent inequality between the haves and have-nots.

Unlike 'development', a concept only applied to the South, environmental issues stretch all the way up from inside and outside anybody's door – be it in a suburban street, a rainforest clearing, or a stretch of African savanna – to the global commons of the biosphere. What everyone does affects 'the environment', and everyone else.

The US, with five per cent of the world's population, consumes 25 per cent of the world's yearly consumption of fossil fuels and emits carbon at a rate of 17.6 tonnes per head – the highest rate among countries with sizeable populations. But the effects of global warming do not confront Americans daily, even if extreme weather events are becoming more common and floods and storm damage more widespread.

The brunt of sea-level change from global warming will be borne by people in densely populated parts of Asia and Africa who live in deltas on which the entire agricultural production of a country depends: the Nile in Egypt, the Brahmaputra and Ganges in Bangladesh, the Mekong in Vietnam. The rate of sea-level rise has recently speeded up, from an average of 1.8 millimeters a year in 1961-2003, to 3.2 millimeters a year from 1993-2010.[6] In critical farmland deltas, even a few millimeters of change significantly increases the risk of catastrophic flood and crop destruction.

Global warming, natural habitat depletion, erosion, submergence, oceans polluted with oil spills and five trillion pieces of plastic: here is a set of issues that imbue the cliché about living in an interdependent global village with real meaning. But achieving a common sense of purpose between countries with different perceptions of threat and at different phases of resource extraction, has proved extremely hard.

Growth-led industrialization and trade remains the favored path to development in countries with aspirations to become card-carrying members of the modern world. They are very unwilling to constrain their development with inhibiting and expensive environmental regulatory regimes, unless the industrialized world is willing to pay.

Meanwhile the North's dilatory efforts to regulate energy consumption do little to encourage Southern governments to control emissions or practise ecological restraint. But since 90 per cent of population growth will take place in their countries, they will have to take a different path to industrialization than that of the North if their environment is to remain habitable. Already, pollution, water and power shortages and traffic congestion are intolerable. Jakarta and Shanghai suffer the world's worst air pollution. Water resources are under special threat.

The rush to growth spurred by globalization has brought development to China, India and other rapidly industrializing countries at an environmental price. While there have recently been carbon emissions drops of 2-3 per cent annually in the US, Europe and Japan, both China and India have been growing their carbon footprints. In 2006, China overtook the US as the largest total emitter, and China's emissions per head now match the EU average.[7] This has come hand in hand with pollution and health crises. The first indications that China might be willing to discuss a cap on emissions finally came in 2013.

Whatever the official reluctance in the South, at the civil society level grassroots green movements have multiplied spectacularly, finding common purpose with Northern counterparts. Campaigns run the gamut from anti-dam movements to fisheries protection and freedom from genetically modified (GM) foods. Some are concerned with air quality from vehicle pollution, water profligacy or consumer waste. Many mind less about what is happening to the planet than about matters of life and death, here and now. Millions of people, especially indigenous groups, are fighting to preserve the habitat they need to survive. For them, 'sustainability' is a deadly serious matter.

A green leap forward?

Of all the attempts to re-energize the 'development' mission in the new millennium, the environmental push has been the most powerful. The campaign against world poverty has effectively been co-opted into the campaign to promote the planet's wellbeing under the 'sustainability' logo.

The conditions of life of billions of people were not on their own capable of igniting worldwide fervor against the doctrine of unfettered growth. Indeed, since growth has apparently conferred a 'developed' lifestyle on millions of previously poor people, whether 'development' is

Smallholder adaptation to climate change

In northern Ghana, where dryland smallholders depend on cassava, the rains are becoming increasingly unreliable. Unpredictable harvests, both for food stores and cash surplus, are a matter of life and death in such communities. The threat of climate change is not experienced as a sudden catastrophe, but as an accumulation of poor seasons declining to a dustbowl.

Around 350 million people currently live on fragile margins in dryland Africa. They are not responsible for the global warming whose effects they have to bear. These communities can be assisted with adaptation and mitigation, if they are brought into a local planning process. Improved crop and fodder production using low water-consumption methods is practicable.

An NGO, Tree Aid, working in northern Ghana talks of 'resilience thinking'. The rural smallholders of dryland Africa and their equivalents elsewhere already know about 'resilience thinking'. To translate this into strategies for 'climate change resilience' can be done, but only by incremental improvements at smallholder level, with their own participation.

nin.tl/NIresilienceblog

pro- or anti-poverty has become confused. Whereas what unchecked growth has done to the environment has become a universal banner under which activism for people and the planet has flourished.

Despite the dispiriting rate of progress on climate change, on other parts of the global commons agenda the international community has made a green leap forward. In our more environmentally conscious age, less polluting and energy-guzzling adaptations of everything from car exhausts to refrigerators and heating systems have emerged. Alternative energy via wind farms and solar panels are here to stay: in the US, jobs in solar already outnumber jobs in coal. 'Ecological' is no longer a freak word but respectably mainstream.

In theory at least, all large projects now have to go through social and environmental hoops and clearance procedures. Where international investors are faced by the realities of what their investments will do, and what genuine compensation packages, heritage conservation and environmental mitigation will cost, at least some are persuaded to stand back. In 2014, Chile cancelled five large dams in the Patagonia region under strong public pressure, and approved new solar and wind farms instead.[8] Elsewhere, things are not so promising. In China and India, huge dam construction is just as popular as ever.

... and 'greenwashing'

Some large companies, including a few oil giants beleaguered by environmentalist protest, have made a lot of noise about 'renewables' and social responsibility, especially after the impression made by Al Gore's Oscar-winning 2006 documentary *An Inconvenient Truth*. But disillusioned activists now protest that big business commitment was only superficial 'greenwashing'. Richard Branson's pledge of $3-billion worth of investment in biotechnology to identify a 'miracle fuel' to replace oil and gas has fallen extremely short.[9] To the despair of environmentalist Jonathon Porritt, the hydrocarbon supremacists have retaken charge at BP and Shell, even though they know that their business model threatens the long-term prospects for humanity.[10] Whenever something else – a war, a Eurozone crisis, oil price fluctuation – distracts attention, the corporate green uniform is conveniently discarded.

The World Business Council on Sustainable Development continues to put forward the view that transnational corporations can espouse environmental concerns without losing competitiveness in national or global markets, and that there are major business opportunities to be seized in building the sustainable world. Their *Action 2020* plan talks of reversing the damage done to ecosystems and moving to a post-industrial low-carbon economy.[11]

The clue to sustainability, according to this vision, lies in a more efficient exploitation of resources until such time as 'miracle fuels' and other technological wizardry come to the rescue. Skeptics scoff at the notion that technology can be used to solve the ecological problems created by technology. Cars are now more fuel-efficient. But fuel efficiency does not solve the problem of exponentially growing traffic. While overall consumption rises, all efficiency can do is to buy time.

Social scientist Wolfgang Sachs points out: 'An ecology of means has to be accompanied by an ecology of ends. The efficiency revolution will remain counterproductive if it is not accompanied by a sufficiency revolution. Nothing is as irrational as running with high speed and with utmost efficiency in the wrong direction.'[12] A sufficiency revolution would mean a cap on growth.

At present, neither North nor South would remotely consider an international agreement on limits to growth, which is what in the end 'sustainability' will have to be about. Naomi Klein believes that today's neoliberal commitment to expanding global markets, shrinking the state, deregulation, and selling off the public domain to a corporate profit-making elite, makes calls for state intervention of the kind required effectively heretical. For the key players on the world stage, 'sustainable' development is more about how to sustain current patterns of excess than the tolerance capacity of the ecosystem or of human societies.

Meanwhile, what has been happening to the sustainability of the livelihoods of those still living partially or entirely off the natural resource base?

Life's essentials: food

At the time of the 1996 World Food Summit, 800 million lives in the world were still threatened by hunger. A target was set: to reduce this figure by half within 20 years. One old-stager was scathing: 'What kind of cosmetic solutions are we going to provide,' thundered Fidel Castro, 'so that 20 years from now there will be 400 instead of 800 million starving people? The very modesty of these goals is shameful.'

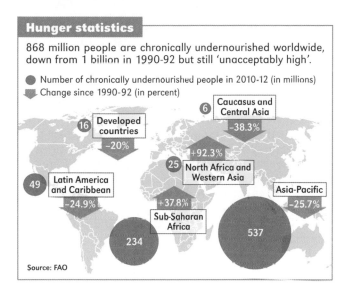

The 20 years are nearly up. And, as we saw in the last chapter, more than 800 million people are still hungry. Yet the Food and Agriculture Organization (FAO) says that the MDG of reducing hunger by half by 2015 is within reach. How? They use a baseline of 1990, and calculate the numbers of undernourished at that time as over one billion. A drop of over 200 million since then is depicted as major progress. This kind of selective use of statistics makes it seem as if hunger is close to being conquered. Yet one in eight people in the South remain chronically underfed.[13]

Hunger, or 'lack of food security', is the quintessential indicator of poverty. To have enough to eat, a household either has to have enough land to grow food, or enough cash to buy it and some reserves for difficult years. Over two-thirds of the world's poorest people are rural[14]; in their case, therefore, the essential issue is access to land for cropping or grazing; if they are landless, to work as labor upon it. Income may be supplemented by micro-enterprises – snack foods, utensils, cloth – forming part of the surrounding economy. This is the kind of economy with its informal mechanisms, tiny margins and mini-transactions, only seen in negatives: too primitive, too inefficient, too vulnerable.

This economy supports hundreds of millions of smallholding families, admittedly in some cases only by the thinnest of margins. But that is not an argument for its destruction. An Oxfam report of 2011 described the global food system as broken, and called for priority to be given to 'small-scale food producers, where the major gains in productivity, sustainable intensification, poverty reduction and resilience can be achieved'.[15] The misallocation of resources, which puts vast amounts of public money for agriculture into agro-industrial farms, should surely be redirected to incremental change in small-scale farming fortunes.

The worst crime against the hungry is the systematic raid on 'under-used' land which started in the early 2000s. Of all the anomalies thrown up by climate change, the spectacle of millions of hectares being removed from the production of food for the hungry so that the North can reduce its carbon footprint (by dubiously effective means) is the most shocking. In the coming decade, biofuel production is expected to increase by 70 per cent, underpinned by government subsidies.[16] A competition between crops to feed people and crops to feed combustion engines raises food prices.

In Honduras, the competition between mouths and tanks fuels a dirty war, with US-backed security forces implicated in the murder, disappearance and intimidation of peasant farmers in dispute with palm-oil magnates. Many farmers have been trying for years to gain the restoration of land coercively transferred to agribusiness companies under a World Bank-funded 'modernization' program. Since a coup in 2009 ended the prospects of a negotiated settlement, more than 100 people have been killed or disappeared, many assassinated by death squads.[17]

Plantations and land grabs

The typical 'development' approach to agricultural investment in the South has always been the creation of large plantations in line with a mechanization, scale-economy model. The 'green revolution' transformation in food crops was all about yields, productivity via fertilizers and pest-resistance, improving irrigation efficiency and 'crop per drop', not about platefuls of something for the hungry to eat. The attention was fixed on the big picture. Crops became assets with which agribusiness corporations played the commodities markets.

While yields kept growing and food prices remained low, warnings fell on deaf ears. But complacency about the global food supply ended after 2008. Many countries that had earlier benefited from prices in minerals and oil did little about food production. They expected to import their food from the globalized supermarket, but suddenly, cereals were not on the shelves. Price hikes on

---

Land grabs

After 2008, when food prices spiked and some countries became seriously alarmed about future food supplies, 'land grabs', especially in Africa, became a hot topic. But reliable information about the deals was hard to find. In 2012, a coalition of NGOs and research groups published a database of deals struck since 2000. An area of 70.2 million hectares (173 million acres) – an area half the size of western Europe – had come under 'new ownership'. New information is constantly added to the database.

Some highlights from the initial report:

- Eastern Africa had the largest number of deals: 310
- Indonesia had given up the largest amount of land to investors: 9.5 million hectares; DR Congo was second, with 8.1 million hectares
- The majority of deals are for agricultural projects (690 deals, 50.2 million hectares); forestry is second (94 deals, 12.7 million hectares)
- Of the agricultural deals, fewer than 30% are for food crops; 20% are for non-food crops such as biofuels and livestock feed.

See landmatrix.org/en/

---

staples in 2008-10 led to political unrest in more than 40 countries, including in the Middle East. Reduction of subsidies on bread was one of the triggers leading to the Arab Spring.

In China, a fifth of the world's population has to be fed from only eight per cent of the world's arable land. Half of this has become degraded by years of unchecked development, urbanization and pollution.[18] The sprawl of tiny farms is giving way to construction, displacing people who have no wish to migrate into the concrete jungle. Large-scale industrialized farming has led to several food-safety disasters: pesticide-soaked fruit, melamine-laced milk. And as incomes rise, eating habits change. Chinese meat consumption has quadrupled in 30 years. In 2014, China scrapped its grain self-sufficiency policy and now relies more on imports. It has also begun to outsource food production abroad, entering into land deals in Africa, Brazil and Argentina.

'Land grabs' by state investors, especially by China, have attracted much negative publicity. But there is something more twisted afoot. After 2008 there was a rush to snap up swathes of land at rock-bottom prices from developing countries keen to cash in on speculation and fear. Like houses bought not for living in, but for capital accumulation, land in Africa is leased on long-term contracts by hedge funds and other investors simply as an asset, against the prospect of future shortage. Many deals have yet to lead to any farming production.

Oxfam points to a 'perfect storm' of demography, scarcity and climate change besetting food prospects for the hungry. The lack of urgent action on global warming means that prices of basic staples – rice, wheat and maize – are set to rise rapidly in the next 20 years. This is bound to hurt the poorest most: their expenditure on food can amount to 60 per cent of household spending. Although rural scarcity gets most of the attention, things are often worse in town. In slums such as those in Kinshasa and Monrovia, many people eat only once a day. Parents eject their children onto the street to beg, steal or prostitute themselves because they cannot afford to feed them.

Filling the world's food basket faces a serious sustainability challenge, independently of the other challenge: who gets to eat from it.

Pressure on water

Food and quality of life prospects are made more complicated by severe stresses on water resources, stresses also exacerbated by growing demand for the rich-world lifestyle – by definition, one of high water consumption.

At present, around 70 per cent of water withdrawals are still for irrigated agriculture. Turkmenistan, a typically arid Central Asian country highly dependent economically on farmland irrigation, is the world's most extravagant user of water: 5,000 cubic meters per person, compared to 20 cubic meters in fertile and rainy Uganda.[19] But the proportions required for manufacturing are rising rapidly, as well as for hydropower and domestic use. There is talk of a global crisis of over-extraction and consumption of water, leading to 'water wars'. By 2050, 40 per cent of the global population are projected to be living in areas subject to severe water stress.[20]

Cities and industries are already competing with agriculture for scarce supplies, while water tables everywhere are dropping, and rivers and aquifers becoming more polluted. The pressures come from water-intensive farming, water-profligate urban lifestyles and reckless attitudes towards wastes. Unless water-use trends change radically, it is unclear how long the world's finite supply of freshwater and natural self-cleansing properties can cope.

Just as there are hundreds of millions of people suffering from food insecurity, there are similar numbers suffering from water insecurity and health-threatening pollution. Never mind the MDG claim of success on this

Pressure on water

In the absence of new policies, freshwater availability will become increasingly strained, with more than 40% of the 2050 population living in water stress areas. Global water demand in terms of water withdrawals is projected to increase by 55%, especially for manufacturing (400%), electricity generation (140%) and domestic use (130%).

Global water demand, 2000 and 2050

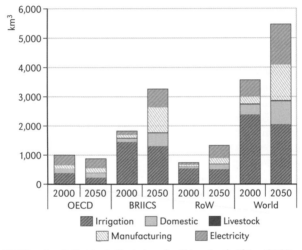

BRIICS = Brazil, Russia, India, Indonesia, China, South Africa; OECD = Organization for Economic Cooperation and Development; ROW = Rest of the World. Rain-fed agriculture not included.

Source: State of the World's Water Report 2014.

front: at the last count 600 million people were without a supply of safe drinking water, and 2.5 billion without proper means of sanitation.[21]

Whenever these matters are internationally discussed, the unsustainability of 'business as usual' regarding patterns of land and water use is endlessly lamented. The numbers of those whose lives are barely sustainable now because of food and water shortages are cited in evidence. But the degree to which 'business as usual' has actually brought about their plight is less well acknowledged. Few really poor people live in lush, irrigated plains. If they do, it is only as the cheapest of labor or in densely settled delta areas such as Bangladesh where holdings are tiny. Over time, most have been squeezed out of productive soils onto arid or semi-arid fringes, or up the slopes of hillsides where erosion is at its worst.

The pressures on such marginal lands quickly denudes them: hunger often goes hand in hand with ecosystems reduced to wastelands because there was no other way to grow a crop. Farmers in Vietnam told inquirers: 'We know that cutting down trees will cause water shortages, but we have no choice. Because we lack food we have to exploit the forest.' Measures introduced to control the loss of woodland further discriminate against those living in wilderness areas. Indigenous people without title become excluded, designated 'encroachers' of their own lands. And it is not the case that such people are museum-exhibit minorities. Environmental archeologist Jared Diamond recently pointed out that not millions but billions of people are still living their lives at least partly according to traditional livelihood norms.[22]

GM – a magic bullet?

Many of the technological and market-oriented solutions put forward to deal with land and water scarcity amount to 'business as usual', only with extras: measures that put tariffs between people and their natural resource base in the name of 'efficiency' and 'management by demand'. The hybrid seeds of Green Revolution fame, and the inputs of fertilizers and pesticides that go with them, are costly to grow and can push small farmers into debt or displacement. Moreover, their effects do not endlessly multiply. Global yields of food crops are now growing only by one per cent, compared to the two per cent that was typical a decade or two ago.

To bring on the next food-production breakthrough, a further revolution is proposed, courtesy of biotechnology.

Claims are made on behalf of genetically modified (GM) new rice varieties: that they will produce 50 per cent higher yields, mature 30-50 days earlier, be more disease- and drought-resistant, and grow without fertilizer or herbicides. They can even be fixed to contain Vitamin A, which would dramatically improve young children's health. Never mind that a handful of green vegetables, without the high-tech costs, would do the same.

When the UN Development Programme (UNDP) announced early in the millennium that it supported GM technology as a way to help those living in poverty, there was an outcry from the non-governmental community. Vandana Shiva, a distinguished Indian environmentalist committed to 'seed freedom' – opposing the imposition of patents and laws to establish corporate monopolies on seeds and prevent farmers from using their own – described the promotion of GM crops as a betrayal of the South, and of the prospects for food security of the poorest sectors of society. According to Shiva: 'Farmers triple their incomes by getting off the chemical treadmill and out of the debt trap created by purchase of costly seeds and chemicals.'[23] Others believe that, at best, GM is a familiar sort of magic-bullet distraction. It diverts attention from kindlier technologies and farming practices that also raise productivity. And it overlooks costs and economic misfit.

The truth is that in no case in history has the intro-duction of this kind of technological innovation favored the poorest in society: on the contrary, it erects barriers between poor people and their resource base. There is too big a gap between the economy in which such people currently operate, and the one in which new seeds, additives and inputs are located. If they accept the package, they risk becoming locked into a technology they can neither afford nor control. If they do not, they get driven or priced out. Those who gain most are those in command of the technology, and of wider agricultural commodity markets: agrochemical companies and landowners who can afford to jump onto the bandwagon and share in its profits.

Sustainable living, viewed from the ground

The preservation of the global commons – climate, ozone, freshwater, oceans – requires international action and its accompaniments: treaties, regulations, incentives and the latest technological inventions. But these have a limited use for promoting sustainable livelihoods based on natural resources.

This is because every location is different. The complex of factors influencing the resource base – topography, geology, soils, water, plants – and people's multiple interactions with it and with each other over its assets, decide whether livelihoods are sustainable or not. If you start from the perspective of the poorest people, you address their specific circumstances.

Robert Chambers, a lifelong advocate of this approach, sees small-scale, sensitive, locally designed and locally managed interventions as ecological and political safeguards against pillage and degradation by commercial interests and the better off. 'Contrary to popular professional prejudice,' he maintains, 'when poor people have secure rights and adequate assets to deal with contingencies, they tend to take a long view, holding on tenaciously to land, protecting trees and seeking to provide for their children. Their time perspective is longer than that of commercial interests concerned with early profits from capital, or of conventional development programs concerned with internal rates of return.'[24]

Once again, it is the non-governmental practitioners with their willingness to spend time and effort exploring existing local systems and traditional technologies who have been in the vanguard of 'sustainable' solutions to the livelihood problems of the poor. They are pioneers, or modernizing rediscoverers, of techniques such as micro-dams, inter-cropping systems, moisture-conserving crop management and rainwater harvesting techniques to make life and food production more secure for the 600 million farming people living in the drylands covering a third of the earth's surface.

Examples of small-scale successful approaches can be quoted from all over the world: rainwater harvesting in India, permaculture in Kenya, small pumps (foot- or fuel-operated) for vegetable irrigation, stone bunds for water catchment in the Sahel. These schemes are similar in that they rely on adapting and improving indigenous technologies and systems of land-water-use management; and that any outside assistance they receive is flexible and low-cost. In all other ways they are unique.

Ecological and social systems are dynamic, and any intervention, to be successful, needs to be tailor-made. Wherever jewels of sustainable development emerge, as with the stone-lined fields of Burkina Faso, soil conservation on the eroded highlands of Nepal, or agro-forestry in Haiti, the development industry instantly calls for 'replicability' and 'scaling up'. But often the idiosyncrasies are themselves the clue.

Localized solutions to the sustainability conundrum that cannot be 'rolled out' like a marketing strategy are often regarded as freakish products of distorted – because socially driven – investment. However, 'replicability' has turned out to be as elusive as the pot of gold at the end of the rainbow and 'scaling up' no easier. An approach relying on stone bunds and low elevations, for example, cannot work where land is steep and there is no natural supply of stones. Any community management system of a resource base has to grow organically in response to day-to-day requirements; its success in one setting does not necessarily mean it can be parachuted onto a thousand more.

Most indigenous small-scale land and water management schemes suffer from a lack of public assistance in the form of credit, subsidized loans, extension services and technical support. Yet these are always available on large-scale irrigation programs that have a far worse track record. Official irrigation statistics for sub-Saharan Africa used not to include land irrigated under traditional methods. When the UN Food and Agriculture Organization corrected its figures to include them, the area rose by 37 per cent.

What about a fresh start?

What is most disturbing in the recent past is that voices insisting on starting where people are at are vanishing from the 'development' discourse, compared with two or three decades ago. Even NGO and civil-society spokespeople have been pushed onto the retreat by the global supremacy of the corporate-bureaucracy nexus.

The distortions in policy – support for grand-slam approaches and openings for agribusiness, and neglect for local forms of sustainable agriculture – have become entrenched despite brave but increasingly sidelined viewpoints. There is acknowledgement that there is no one route to sustainable development. But the establishment is not willing to contemplate the true implications of what it takes to integrate the two concepts, including 'limits to growth'.

Up to now, the kind of reforms that would open up the prospects of poor communities achieving their own forms of sustainable resource-base management have not attracted much support. We have to hope that, given the suicide rate among indebted farmers and the boiling anger in many rural communities, the structural inhibitions and obduracy of vested interests will give way. Otherwise, the widespread misery of farmers and urban slum-dwellers may find increasingly dangerous expression.

Since the concept of sustainability was first invented, much that is valuable for poor communities has been done in its name. But nothing like enough. And much of what has been done is a frantic rearguard action against the continuing invasion of their fragile resource base. Many poor communities see further threats on their horizons from corporate or government predators, and from floods, droughts or other outcomes of global warming.

Those who heralded with enthusiasm the new era of sustainable development feel deeply disillusioned. But most of the failures are political, and have little to do with the environment at all. So it is to the politics of development that we turn next.

1 Barbara Ward and René Dubois, *Only One Earth*, WW Norton, 1972. **2** Most demographic statistics are from World Population Prospects, UN Population Division, esa.un.org/wpp **3** World Urbanization Prospects 2014 Revision, UN Economic and Social Affairs, nin.tl/urbanization-prospects **4** Stephen Emmott, *Ten Billion*, Penguin 2013. **5** Naomi Klein, *This changes everything: Capitalism vs the Climate*, Penguin 2015. **6** IPCC data, Assessment Reports of 2007 and 2014: nin.tl/IPCClatest; nin.tl/IPCClatest2 **7** Adam Vaughan and Tania Branagan, 'China to limit carbon emissions for first time', *The Guardian*, 3 Jun 2014, nin.tl/Chinaemissionspledge **8** Data from International Rivers Campaign, internationalrivers.org/blogs/227-3 **9** 'Sticky business', edited extract from Naomi Klein's *This changes everything*, *The Guardian*, 13 Sep 2014, nin.tl/Kleinongreenwashing **10** Jonathon Porritt, *The Guardian*, 15 Jan 2015, nin.tl/PorrittonBigOil **11** See their website wbcsd.org/home.aspx **12** Quoted in *Green Politics*, ed Anil Agarwal, Sunita Narain and Anju Sharma, CSE and Earthscan, 1999. **13** *The State of Food Insecurity in the World*, FAO, 2014, p 8, fao.org/publications/sofi/en **14** *The Rural Poverty Report 2011*, IFAD, ifad.org/rpr2011/report **15** *Growing a better future*, Oxfam 2011, p 8, oxfam.org/grow **16** Shengan Fan, 'People first: green goals should not override ending hunger', *The Guardian*, 6 May 2014. **17** Nina Lakhani, 'Honduras and the dirty war fuelled by the west's drive for clean energy', *The Guardian*, 7 Jan 2014. **18** Jonathan Kaiman, 'China's rural dilemma: crops or concrete?' *The Guardian*, 16 Feb 2015. **19** *UN World Water Development Report 2009*, UNESCO, p 99, nin.tl/UNESCOwater **20** UN World Water Development Report 2014, p 24, nin.tl/UNESCOwater2014 **21** UNESCO International Hydrological Program, Water Security, nin.tl/UNESCOwatersecurity **22** Jared Diamond, *The World Until Yesterday*, Penguin, 2012, p 7. **23** Vandana Shiva, 'Open letter to Oxfam', and *Water Wars: Privatization, Pollution and Profit*, South End Press, 2002. **24** Robert Chambers, 'Sustainable rural livelihoods', in *The Greening of Aid*, ed Czech Conroy and Miles Litvinoff, Earthscan and IIED, 1988.

6 Development is political

The political nature of development is often ignored. Yet any transformation in society requires a political process. Solidarity with the poor has inevitable political overtones, as those on the ground are fully aware. Where development victimizes certain groups, it engenders disaffection – some of which is expressed in violent and extremist terms. People's movements in the South are engaged in a new politics of nonviolent resistance to neoliberal policies. But as a unifying global cause, 'development' is damaged goods.

When the crusade for development was launched, its context was unequivocally geopolitical: this was a grand international project to enable newly independent countries to embrace economic progress and bind them into alliance with the West. Thus aid packages were based on many considerations other than need – especially the building of strategic and trading partnerships. However, the internal dynamics of the mission were not seen as political – rather, as technocratic.

'Development' had little to do with politicians, still less with political scientists; it was a matter for economists, engineers and planners. Where poor people were concerned, welfarist and humanitarian perceptions ruled, and the task was seen as mopping up politically innocent distress. When social concerns won the right to be viewed as developmental too, the provision of education and healthcare was equally non-political, about building human capital and wellbeing. After this was achieved, a mature and democratic political system would emerge. Few considered that poverty reduction was, itself, a highly political process, and that no policy to promote it could be delivered without structural social change.

On their side, the IMF/World Bank and UN bodies were rigorously bound not to interfere in the internal politics of sovereign member states. So any mission under their auspices must be one from which all taint of politics was extruded. What might politically result from any transfer of resources, and whether such transfers could, or should, have a political purpose were subjects beyond the pale. The only political issue these inter-governmental bodies attended to was that of not taking sides: staying 'above the divide' in any dispute between states or parties within them. In the post-Cold War world, so embroiled have military, political and humanitarian initiatives become that this principle has been compromised. Transnational corporations have assumed the role of 'above the political divide' – but in a very different way.

Keeping development co-operation tied firmly to issues of human and country disadvantage may have been an act of international self-delusion, but it had advantages. During the Cold War, the idea that aid, human rights promotion or co-operation for development could be politically neutral and entirely humanitarian in motive was greeted with skepticism in the Sino-Soviet bloc. Today, it is greeted with skepticism everywhere.

Tackling root causes

While Northern governments masked their use of development aid for political and strategic purpose behind a cloak of neutrality, the more progressive NGO players viewed the political context of development very differently. It soon became obvious to them that tackling the root causes of poverty was an inherently political business. And they embraced it. The hope of bringing about self-improvement and social change made the goal of development preferable to pouring money into welfare.

In the early, naive days, the idea of development was encapsulated by a widely repeated proverb: 'Give a man a fish, and you feed him for a day. Teach him to fish, and you feed him for life.' But knowing how to fish often turned out to be the least of his (or her) problems. The river might be polluted and the catch depleted; the trees from which boats were built felled by loggers, or the right to fish granted to others with powerful patrons and larger boats. Along the coast, illegal trawlers might be hoovering up the local catch on an industrial scale. The 'knowledge transfer' needed was not 'how to fish', but how to organize, bargain collectively, expose corrupt officials and film fishing-boat marauders to get them arrested and fined.[1]

An extreme case in point is that of Somalia. After the collapse of government in the 1990s, the uncontrolled plunder of fish stocks by foreign trawlers off the 3,000-kilometer coast around the Horn of Africa was a driver for the emergence of Somali piracy.[2] High-seas boats from South Korea, Japan and Spain enjoyed a free-for-all among the tuna and sardine shoals, freezing out local boats. Now that Somali piracy has been brought under control, reinforcement comes from international patrols of the coast keeping foreign trawlers out, while re-equipping Somali fishers.

How could power struggles be removed from fishing, around Africa's coasts or anywhere else? Interventions to support livelihoods not only have to fit economic and social realities, but also to contend with politics. If they do not, vested interests destroy them or co-opt every benefit to themselves. Even UN Secretary-General Ban Ki-moon has concluded that this can induce marginalized people whose human rights and dignity have been abused to react with extreme acts of violence.[3]

Control over resources

Why has what was originally seen as a benign process, one seen as quintessentially 'right', become so contested? The answer is straightforward. Development requires new configurations in the use and distribution of resources of land, money and human labor. These are bound to entail disputes among individuals and groups, which can only be sorted out by a political process.[4]

Conflicts over resources

There are many examples where competition for minerals has been responsible for fuelling conflict. Mining organizations may become complicit in hostilities by trading in conflict resources, such as diamonds, timber, minerals, or poppy seeds for opium. The most prominent case of a region entirely destabilized and impoverished by a conflict resource war is Eastern Congo.

Most countries in the South that are dependent on the export of primary commodities such as fossil fuels and minerals, especially in circumstances of inequality, instability, and the absence of effective government, are plagued by conflict, corruption, environmental damage, human rights violations, poverty and extreme discrimination against indigenous groups.

Mining clashes in Latin America 2013

Mexico 28

Colombia 12

Chile 32

Brazil 20

Argentina 26

Peru 34

In the **Madre de Dios** region of the **Peruvian Amazon** the recent gold rush accelerated deforestation from **2,166 hectares** a year before 2008 to **6,145 hectares** after 2008 when gold prices soared. It has also led to widespread **mercury pollution**, affecting the entire food chain.

In **Chile** in 2010, **25%** of the country was being explored or mined. Mining uses **37%** of the country's electricity but creates only **1%** of all jobs, most of which are poorly paid and insecure.

Source: *New Internationalist* 470, March 2014: Blessing or curse: the pitfalls of resource wealth.

The way in which command over resources makes or breaks a country's prospects is illustrated most tellingly by the fact that several modern conflicts – Afghanistan, South Sudan, DR Congo, Liberia – have been financed by the control and illegal marketing of natural resources such as oil, diamonds, timber, opium and minerals. In other circumstances, such as takeover of land for mines or plantations, the exertion of such control may be 'legitimate', exercised in the name of the national good; but the experience of the excluded may be little different.

When pressure on natural resources leads to discrimination against the least powerful and the poorest, as it invariably does, enabling them to make permanent improvements in their circumstances will be problematic. The notion of an expanded cake from which largesse may be neutrally distributed is a fiction. Confrontations – with landowners, party bosses, those with economic or bureaucratic muscle – are inevitable, as activists will universally bear out.

Nonetheless, the illusion that they can steer clear of politics is one to which many donors and technocrats cling. They point to regulatory systems and compensation requirements which are never delivered, ignoring the pusillanimity of politicians, officials and justice systems. They claim, more insistently even than trans-national companies, that the state of the poor is not an outsider's affair, and that they cannot take sides. How to promote 'justice' without taking sides is unclear.

Within democratic societies, there are mechanisms for negotiating changes in access to resources. They may not always work well, but at least they are there. In non-democratic societies, or in societies where the hierarchy of power is so entrenched and socially legitimized as to override a democratic veneer, it is almost impossible for weaker groups to assert their right to a share of any cake. Few countries in the developing world enjoy a consolidated democracy, either within their formal political structures or in the rest of their institutions.

Inequality and poverty reinforce each other

Where inequality of power, wealth and opportunity exists, improvements in services for human development such as education and health invariably favor those who are better off, reinforcing the likelihood of deepening inequality in the next generations.

The case of under-five mortality in Uganda 2000 and 2011

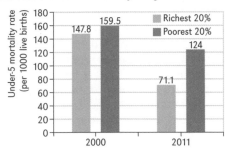

The case of educational access in Ethiopia: who does not go to school?

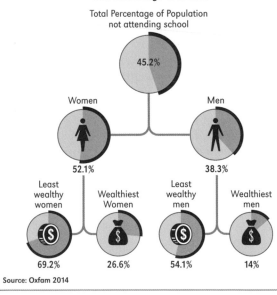

Source: Oxfam 2014

In Latin America, modern political models were superimposed on pre-modern societies and markets at independence; representative democracy did not grow from organic and socially inclusive processes – on the contrary the exercise of power has been predatory and extractive.[5] The same goes for most of Asia and all of Africa. Governments may be elected, but that does not make society's institutions inclusive and redistributive, let alone democratic. Many governments, not only in the South, are run by powerful individuals whose only motive for being in office is personal graft.

When development is introduced in circumstances of gross inequality, it too will suffer from gross inequality and, in all likelihood, reinforce it. If there is a program to build power stations, drill boreholes, or construct clinics, politics will play a part in decisions about where they are put, and who owns and runs them. All the way down from the national planning commission, to the district council, the village, even to the household, the exercise of power decides who gains first or most from any service. New amenities will not bypass the homes or communities of the influential on their way to weaker ones. The most a countervailing force can do is to make sure they don't stop at the influential, that they do aim to reach the poorer eventually.

When development as a purely economic process first came under fire, some commentators began to highlight the political dimension, without acknowledging the inherently political nature of what they were suggesting. They called for 'growth with equity' and 'redistribution'. The problem was that, unless a national government was politically committed to equitable development – which in most cases was expressed as socialism and therefore an ideological anathema in the West – there was little fertile ground for such ideas. The countries of the Western alliance might deplore military dictatorships and one-party states, but the last thing they would do was encourage leftist opposition. The destabilization and destruction of socialist leaders in the South remained central to US foreign policy.

The rise of people's movements

While the international establishment kept politically aloof, progressive NGOs and human rights activists complained vociferously about the raw deal poor countries and poor people were getting. In the UK, such organizations ran a protracted battle to be allowed to campaign on these issues, and still get threatened with loss of charitable status for behaving 'politically'. Their attempts in the field to help poor people exert control over their lives increasingly produced political dilemmas. These emerged earliest in military-dominated Central and South America in the 1970s.

In northeast Brazil, for example, poverty's basics – low income, low skills, illiteracy, hunger and ill-health – interacted with violent oppression against indigenous groups in the Amazonian rainforests, dispossession of peasant lands and continuing forms of rural slavery. Recife, the regional capital, was a crucible of radical thinking on the continent and home of the internationally renowned Archbishop Helder Camara: 'When I give food to the poor, they call me a saint. When I ask why the poor have no food, they call me a communist.'

Under the inspirational leadership of priests, local leaders and disenchanted professionals, a number of grassroots movements emerged. Many were intent on improving members' agricultural output, literacy and health – an impeccable menu for social development; but they set about this by mobilizing and 'empowering' people to act on their own behalf. Demands for access to resources were threatening to ruling oligarchies. The progressive arm of the church became the seat of protest about the condition of those living in poverty, and all the rhetoric and sometimes the armed violence of anti-communism was used against them.

External partners who supported pro-poor activities

in Latin America found that communities that had transformed themselves with help from external NGOs were being deliberately undermined, even massacred, during civil wars in Guatemala, Nicaragua and El Salvador. In many countries, including Mexico, Colombia and Peru, it was impossible to avoid the politics of development. The same applied in southern Africa, where liberation from racist oppression did not arrive until the 1990s.

For development activists, hard choices had to be made: 'empowerment' could invite state repression. Without empowerment, support from the international community propped up the forces of oppression. In such settings, championing poor people had to mean opposing the state. The same holds true today, except that the oppressors are less easy to identify. Some claiming to liberate the poor have turned out to be oppressors in disguise.

New forms of liberation struggle

As the Cold War drew to an end, as walls fell and old barriers crumbled, the emergence of grassroots organizations in the South began in earnest. These have since become a force in development at the popular level.

Some began as actions to enable poor people to exert control over resources they needed. The Self-Employed Women's Association (SEWA) in Gujarat, India, for example, enabled women trading in the informal sector – 94 per cent of working women in India are self-employed – to avoid dependency on moneylenders and resist police fines. SEWA, with its micro-finance and other programs, has since gone from strength to strength and now has nearly two million members.[6]

Other people's organizations, also in India, mounted resistance to large projects or destructive resource extraction. These included the Chipko movement in the Himalayas, which tried to stop the felling of trees and the erosion of farming land. The Narmada Bachao Andolan, formed in 1985, protested – still protests – the impact of large dams and the dispossession and ecological damage they cause in fertile and heavily populated river valleys.[7] Victims of development disaster – the thousands of people killed or otherwise affected by a gas leak in Bhopal in 1984, for example – also began to organize.

In Brazil there was the rubber-tappers' union, a collective of associations under their leader Chico Mendes (later assassinated), resisting forest clearances that ruined their livelihoods. In 1993, small farmers' representatives from many parts of the world formed La Via Campesina to claim a voice in food and agricultural policy. This international association now comprises 164 member organizations in 73 countries, representing 200 million small farmers.[8]

The phenomenon of social movements in the South among workers, farmers, slum-dwellers, fishers, and others trying to resist development destruction politicized development from a new perspective.[9] These movements were authentic expressions of people's will and action on their own behalf, not offshoots of the international development industry or other formal structures. They generated resources, managed activities, developed policies and protested injustice from their own support base. Northern solidarity groups – the International Rivers Network, Human Rights Watch, Greenpeace, Environmental Justice Foundation – provided modest support and platforms to enable campaigners to reach an international audience.

Many movements represented the closest thing to a 'political' opposition practically allowed in their own countries. They not only expressed dissent with the existing order, but also provided some basis for a developmental and democratic alternative. Although most used leftwing vocabulary and precepts, they did not align with political parties. Even in democratic societies, they reject party politics; they tend to see conventional political routes to 'right wrongs' as corrupt, ineffective and in league with big power and big money.

Civil society takes the stage

The early post-Cold War years felt like a new development dawn. There was, first, the 'peace dividend' which, it was thought, would enable aid to flow. More importantly, a tide of freedom was sweeping into the furthest reaches of the world. The struggle for liberty in the former USSR and in southern Africa, and the demand for development 'for the people and by the people', must surely be two sides of the same coin.

The downfall of Pinochet in Chile, of Mobutu in Zaire (DR Congo), the ascendancy of Nelson Mandela in South Africa, the end to civil conflicts in Central America – all were ushering democracy into places from which it had long been absent. In a world released from the stranglehold of superpower stand-off, tyrants would no longer be supported as bulwarks against the communist foe and democratic forces would surely be allowed to flourish.

The NGOs revelled in their new legitimacy as manifestations of 'civil society'. Their success at mobilizing people behind a localized process of change was lauded, and even their smallest organized expressions were brought within the loop of development policy and practice. 'Civil society' was congratulated for succeeding where bureaucracy had failed, and its role in the new world order was officially welcomed. Alongside the opening up of markets, deregulation and privatization – about which civil society was understandably wary – ran an agenda for political reform: calls for democracy and 'good governance', of which civil society approved.

In their new capacity, NGOs in North and South were now partners of governments and accepted in forums where policy was discussed. But there were suspicions on both sides. From governments, there was still often an attitude of lofty patronage towards sometimes polemical, sometimes naive, sometimes self-seeking, cuckoos in the nest. On their side, civil-society institutions were unconvinced by the economic agenda and unsure that the political one amounted to much. They also risked loss of independence by their admittance to the 'development club'.

Sadly, the potential for partnerships between governments and people's organizations in the evolution of alternative, genuinely participatory forms of development – building bridges between traditional and modern ways of doing things – was not all it seemed. Where the forward march of transnational vested interests was under challenge, the forces of civil society were labelled counterproductive. Their advocacy of an up-front anti-poverty and environmentalist agenda was disdained.

The official view, even among many donor governments, was that NGOs should help lead civil society down the primrose path of assent to the dominant political and economic model, and salve the wounds of those who unfortunately fell off the edge. Movements such as the Zapatistas in Mexico, who rose up against laws that ended their indigenous system of landowning, were not seen as outriders of a new development order, but as rebels plain and simple.

Participation and empowerment

In the early 2000s, human-development momentum was still growing. Apart from the anti-poverty agenda of the MDGs, the international apparatus continued to express concern about civil-society inclusion, and even incorporated quasi-political vocabulary in their policies. There was a need for 'participation', for decisions to be made 'at the lowest appropriate level'. Development required people's empowerment, and 'democratization' was a precondition.

Amartya Sen, the Nobel Laureate economist, was the doyen of this idea, writing of 'development as freedom'. Development required: 'The removal of major sources of unfreedom: poverty as well as tyranny, poor economic opportunities as well as systematic social deprivation, neglect of public facilities as well as intolerance or over-activity of repressive states.'[10] Only where these 'freedoms' were assured was it possible for people to live productively in such a way as to promote their own, and wider, human development.

Today this sounds decidedly unreal. In the immediate post-Cold War euphoria, as earlier during the post-colonial buzz, everything seemed possible. But when it came to the crunch, it was hard to see how the international community would bring on the 'freedoms' and remove the 'unfreedoms' described by Sen, or whether they were just garlanding their stock agenda with new vocabulary. They tiptoed round the edge of the real politics of development – control over resources, landowning patterns, marginalization, livelihood security and decision-making power.

In fact, 'participation' had captured adherents not because it would rearrange power, but because it had useful management, administrative and cost-recovery characteristics. Everyone knew that many development projects had floundered because people had been left out, and that where they were allowed to join in, much more was achieved with less. The same reasoning was now applied to 'empowerment', 'democratization' and 'decentralization'. These would all make development not only more 'effective and efficient', but also more 'equitable and sustainable'.

But could such purposes be realized on the ground? For that to happen, all the permutations of problems facing people trying to make a living in situations stacked against them have to be addressed.

The new rhetoric: governance

That such issues are not addressed is, at heart, a political issue. There is, of course, an international or 'global' dimension; but the main dynamics are in the countries and communities where people live.

For people whose livelihoods are at issue, things are not much improved by a new set of development catch phrases. Where their problems are addressed, it is often by a process of rearguard action against practices of neglect or exclusion. This rarely happens unless some organization – people's movement, union, or council – pushes for it. Unless somebody knows how to interact with a particular bureaucracy, gain access to resources and negotiate obstructions, governance agendas are futile.

Many talk about creating an 'enabling environment', but laws and policies decreed from on high often enable very little. Many individuals of amazing courage function in a profoundly disabling environment.

In some instances, the structure of regular programs and the types of inputs – basic health and education services, for example – ensure that some benefits reach those on the outer edge of society. But most of the inter-national commitment to the 'enabling environment' and other such concepts has been rhetorical. How can they be meaningfully delivered in highly inequitable societies where power over people and resources is entrenched in the hands of an elite? The 'good governance' agenda is mostly about standards of efficiency relating to the existing way of doing things, not about serious realloca-tions of power.

Good governance usually involves doing things more cost-effectively and accountably, and bowing in the direction of certain social and environmental policy norms. It can also mean encouraging governments to take action against extremists who might be tempted to take up 'terror'. Rarely does it put people in control of resources or enable them to influence the structures surrounding them – or if it does, only on a very small scale, and around such issues as garbage removal, not around land tenure or conflict.

In a few contexts there have been successful challenges to existing power structures. One is gender. Women have pointed out that their exclusion from education, training and employment has negative economic effects for a country, and that, unless patriarchal power over their lives is reduced, nothing will change. If women are to participate in development, a more equal distribution of political as well as economic power is needed. For women's groups in Africa, Asia and Latin America, 'empowerment' is not just about gaining access to education, credit or childcare services. It is about protection against sexual harassment and exploitation, and this demands sufficient influence on local leaders to induce community sanctions against male violence and abuse.

On behalf of women, children and, to a lesser extent, indigenous groups, there has been some institutional willingness to take up political cudgels. The way this has been done, however, is less through the language of politics than through the language of human rights.

The ascent of rights

During the Cold War, the pursuit of rights at the international level was submerged. Any association between rights and development was denied. 'Freedom from hunger' or 'freedom from poverty' are not rights that could be attained by legislation anyway. The fact that 'justice' could not be present where people had no access to education, healthcare, a decent diet, or a productive livelihood was unfortunate, but development would have to provide these before universal rights to equity and justice could be meaningfully claimed.

The end of East-West confrontation came at a time when this position was under challenge. Development was not taking care of these problems, and instead was often precipitating deprivations of 'freedom': conflict, forced migration, child abuse and exploitation. The 'human needs' argument for development was too weak. A much broader interpretation of rights than liberty and freedom of expression should now be brought to development's aid. Inequalities would be challenged, and the rights of the excluded upheld by laws and international treaties.

The first human rights instrument to legitimize the new thrust was the 1989 UN Convention on the Rights of the Child. This treaty, which achieved near-universal ratification, combined social and economic with civil and political rights. The rights of children to survival, health and education were enshrined in international law alongside their rights to non-discrimination, freedom from exploitation and to have their voices heard. All children had these rights which states had sworn to uphold, and this had implications for public spending, law enforcement and criminal justice – implications few

Ratification of human rights treaties

Since the 1948 Universal Declaration of Human Rights, a number of human rights treaties have been agreed by the UN General Assembly and subsequently passed into international law. Most countries have ratified most of them, but some have ratified very few, notably the US, Bhutan, Burma, many small island countries, and Somalia.

Report card on ratification of six key Conventions
(Universal ratification = **195** countries)

1. Convention on the Rights of the Child (CRC) 1989:
193 country parties; only two exceptions: Somalia and USA

2. Convention on the Elimination of all forms of Discrimination Against Women (CEDAW) 1979:
187 country parties; among those not ratified: Iran, Sudan, and the Holy See.

3. Convention on the Elimination of all forms of Racial Discrimination (CERD) 1965:
175 country parties including USA; among those not ratified: Angola, Burma, S Korea, Malaysia, Singapore.

4. Covenant on Civil and Political Rights (CCPR) 1966:
167 country parties; among those not ratified: China, Cuba, Ethiopia, Oman, Saudi Arabia, UAE.

5. Covenant on Economic, Cultural and Social Rights (CECSR) 1966:
160 country parties; among those not ratified: Belize, Botswana, Haiti, Mozambique, Qatar.

6. Convention against Torture (CAT) 1984:
153 country parties; among those not ratified: Bahamas, Central African Republic, Eritrea, Gambia, India, Jamaica, Papua New Guinea, Sudan, Tanzania.

Source: Office of the High Commissioner for Human Rights, 2013.

governments had anticipated because children are not supposed to be political beings.

The new rights-based agenda had tremendous appeal: trying to make countries live up to rights they had signed up to opened up possibilities on behalf of many discriminated groups. 'Protection' under human rights legislation became another arm of development action. Forms of abuse or discrimination based on sex or gender – rape, girl infanticide, female genital mutilation, trafficking – were affirmed as full-scale abuses of human rights. A UN Declaration was also agreed on the 'human right to development', but this was too amorphous to gain traction.

A shifting framework

Championship of rights has since been increasingly seen as the basis for rectifying inequalities and injustice. Instead of depending on the good will of development policymakers, activists and victim groups have recourse to international law – that their governments have ratified   in trying to get things changed. International organizations feel able to protest rights violations with fewer inhibitions about interfering in sovereignty or cultural practices than before.

The shift to rights as the framework for development action is welcomed by citizen movements in the South. No longer is the championship of rights left to Amnesty International and a handful of specialist organizations; rights have become a common currency. Advocacy for legal change and recourse to the courts are increasingly used as remedies for developmental injustice, especially in South Asia. Campaigning techniques, particularly since the rise of social media, have helped bring out into the open issues which governments prefer to brush under the carpet – slavery, for example, and human trafficking. Southern activists welcome international outcries over rights: it lends their own efforts credibility with politicians, officials and the justice system.

The rights agenda has an edge over the wellbeing agenda when it comes to advocacy on behalf of poor people. But the capacity of international action to make a difference where it matters is necessarily limited. Many governments routinely flout people's rights while signing up to international treaties demanding the opposite. Apart from the International Criminal Court – which can only process a handful of high-profile cases – there is no way to bring perpetrators to book internationally: exposure and 'shaming' are the only weapons. International partners in development programs often fail to notice the everyday discrimination and rights evasion occurring under their noses. And developing-country governments complain that they do not have the resources to put an effective rights regime instantly into place.

Rights is a key development discourse, even if much of the attention has to be rhetorical. Rights fulfilment cannot occur in environments where the rule of law and regular administration barely penetrate – as is the case for most people in poor areas of the South. It is also the case that, since the world became unnerved by 'terror', the rights and democracy agenda has lost ground. Civil-society groups with radical programs are cold-shouldered. Protest against the dominant neoliberal paradigm has become suspect. The surveillance state, the meltdown of the Arab Spring, and the advent of 'austerity' have helped deflate the currency of rights.

Waves of resistance

This does not mean that resistance to the false development promise of neoliberalism is dead. The original blow was struck in November 1999, when 50,000 people gathered in Seattle to disrupt a new round of World Trade Organization (WTO) talks on trade liberalization. With Southern delegates also disaffected, negotiations collapsed and a new international political movement was born.

The vast majority of protesters were trying peacefully

to influence discussions that they believed had no democratic legitimacy and whose intended outcome – to further promote the globalization of the world economy – would impoverish people and the planet. But reaction and counter-reaction became violent. Subsequent international meetings of this kind – the G8, World Economic Forum, WTO trade talks, annual meetings of the World Bank and IMF – were threatened by mass protest and had to be located in fortress-like settings.

Mass protests against land grabbers and other oppressors are becoming more commonplace in marginal areas of Asia and Latin America. In India, a National Alliance of People's Movements with over 100 member organizations resists the onslaught conducted by economic liberalization against people's lands, livelihoods and shanty settlements. In February 2015, they led a major protest against a new ordinance promulgated by Narendra Modi's BJP government which arbitrarily rescinded key provisions of the 2013 Land Acquisition Act, including that requiring 70-per-cent farmer consent.[11]

Globalization is engineering the integration of India's economy with the global economy on terms devised by Northern bankers and corporations, with which their own business leaders, bureaucrats and politicians connive. Their resistance underlines the contradiction at the core of global economic advance: the existing strategy for mass prosperity comes at the cost of exacerbating poverty for millions. This amounts to a redistribution of wealth and power which builds, rather than reduces, inequality, leading to political confrontation. The task for sympathizer NGOs is to try to 'strengthen the poor so that they have some greater opportunity of fashioning life in their favor. This is not a leftwing agenda or a rightwing agenda – it is a justice agenda.' So says Michael Taylor, a former Director of Christian Aid.[12]

Transnational corporations exert increasing economic control over the resource base, but feel no sense of moral obligation or empathy towards the poor communities who live off it. They express surprise and disbelief that the 'development' they bring is unwelcome. Even organizations that ought to be in solidarity show an extraordinary detachment. In the words of an official of the UN Food and Agriculture Organization (FAO), people displaced from their lands are 'variable factors of off-farm production', not families who have lost their all.[13]

The outcry globalization and its inequalities has evoked shows that the grand 'economic reform' agenda is in fact a political project. Those who resist are, in their different ways, rejecting the contemporary form of development. Some see their campaigns as a renaissance. 'Occupy' movements in London and New York protesting the extreme inequality of today's distribution of wealth and power are manifestations of protest with a similar agenda.

The problem is that resistance is anarchic in the political sense of the term: without political leaders, without a manifesto, without a common platform or plan. In most countries, in the North but especially in the South, they function outside the existing structure of organized politics – which they distrust. They are stating clearly what they do not want, and illustrating within their own structures a more humane, ecologically sound and democratic way of being. But it is hard to see how they can effect a major transformation of policy and practice without assaulting the current citadels of power by an extensive political project of their own.

Since 2001, these alternative apostles have come together every year to hold their own World Social Forums. These are loosely framed meetings for the exchange of experience. There is no shared agenda of building organized power.[14]

Every now and again comes some positive sign of successful popular objection to the current mainstream: Morales in Bolivia, Chávez in Venezuela; Otpor! in Serbia, and anti-austerity movements in Europe such as Syriza in Greece and Podemos in Spain. Maybe Syriza's

2015 election triumph will prove a turning-point. But the failed outcome of the Arab Spring, the misery that is Palestine, and the horrifying success of 'Islamic State' and Boko Haram have dealt a blow to the reputation of popular uprising elsewhere.

Politically, the cause of international development as a movement in solidarity with the world's poor appears to have failed. Perhaps, to echo the central thesis of Thomas Piketty's account of capital and inequality, only the 20th-century experience of two world wars and the pressure exerted in the post-colonial world by the existence of a strong socialist sphere with military and political clout allowed the idea of 'development' as a potentially equalizing force to carry weight for so long. The re-emergence of a level of inequality not seen since the 19th century has been accompanied by the re-emergence of big philanthropy with the likes of Gates and Soros taking the place of the Rockefellers and Fords of bygone years. Could the mission be part of the problem, not the solution?

1 See ejfoundation.org on West African fisher pirates, 8 Mar 2015. **2** Ishaan Tharoor, 'How Somalia's Fishermen Became Pirates', *Time*, 18 Apr 2009, nin.tl/Timesomalipirates **3** Interview with Ban Ki-moon by Judy Woodruff, PBS NewsHour, 19 Feb 2015, un_wire@smartbrief.com **4** Adrian Leftwich, *States of Development*, Polity Press, 2000. **5** Daron Acemoglu and James A Robinson, *Why Nations Fail*, Profile Books, 2012. **6** SEWA newsletter, Jan 2014, nin.tl/SEWAnewsletter **7** See nin.tl/Narmadastory **8** nin.tl/aboutViaCampesina **9** *Social Movements in the Global South*, ed Sara C Motta and Alf Gunvald Nilsen, Palgrave MacMillan, 2011. **10** Amartya Sen, *Development as Freedom*, Oxford University Press, 1999. **11** See nin.tl/landseizureIndia **12** BBC Radio 4, 8 Mar 2015, item on 70th anniversary of Christian Aid. **13** John Madeley, *Hungry for trade*, Zed Books, 2000. **14** https://fsm2015.org/en

7 Where next?

After trying to work out what goes on in the name of 'development', it is tempting to echo those who regard the mission as defunct. However, neither the concept nor the work carried out in its name are likely to vanish. Some activists have abandoned the quest for 'development' in favor of 'justice', sharpening the focus on equal opportunity and non-discrimination. Whatever happens next, those this quest for a better life is supposed to benefit should become partners in the process.

At the outset of this book, a central dilemma was posed. How could a process – 'development' – that was meant to be synonymous with poverty reduction have been subverted in such a way as to reinforce the poverty of millions of people?

The dilemma remains. Too often, the pursuit of development fails to address the contradictions between its expressed purpose and its actual effects. Whatever positive gains some actions achieve, others drive millions of people into misery and reduce women and children into marketed objects of servitude. They also banish the voices of ordinary people from debate, violate human rights and inflict losses on natural systems. Although development has brought some poor countries rich-world membership, vast numbers of their inhabitants – notwithstanding their better chances of surviving infancy and longer life expectancy – have been effectively left out. Instead of closing gaps between rich and poor, development has widened them.

Under these circumstances, it is tempting to join the ranks of those who have already announced the demise of the development idea, dismantled its underlying economic theory, or dismissed it as a myth.[1] But powerful as such polemic may be, it is hard to opt out when the development industry is in such rude health.

Despite decades of dashed hopes and increasing public skepticism, aid budgets are up. In the UK, a Conservative government passed a law in early 2015 asserting that 0.7 per cent of GNI must annually be spent on ODA – no other budgetary sector is similarly protected. Instead of retreating in the face of confusion, the development business is flourishing; even banks and corporations are joining in as if an assault on poverty is just where they belong.

More analyses of development's various subsets – including obscurantist intellectual exercises of spurious relevancy – are churned out by the day. More consultants ponder 'knowledge transfer', 'multidimensional poverty measurement' and 'theories of change'. New collaborative bodies meet in Rome, Geneva, Nairobi or New York and pronounce on everything from genetic modification to water security, violence against girls to disaster preparedness. More and more privileged, well off people who have never set foot in the apocryphal 'village' or urban slum gain a living from the development business; even a character in the top UK radio soap opera studies 'international development', anticipating a well-paid job.[2]

At the purely semantic level, the term 'development' is very difficult to drop. Even if it has become 'a concept of monumental emptiness' (Wolfgang Sachs' verdict), the word is hard to replace. As the descriptor of a project to improve sanitation or spread contraception, 'global justice' does not work. The term 'development' has become ingrained in economic language, academic discourse and humanitarian endeavor. In default of some better terminological alternative, we will go on using the one we have.

Unless, that is, we abandon the whole rich world/ poor world divide altogether, and decide that agendas for delivering justice or ending inequality should be universal. No more global deals between North and South, in which the agenda is set in the North, funded by the North, and carried out in and by the South, against performance targets not applied in richer countries where inequalities may be rife. Instead of 'development goals', 'universal goals'; instead of universal access to basic services in poor countries, universal access to basic services in all countries.[3] That would be a great step forward, and one that 'justice' suggests the mission should become – if not immediately, in due course.

Living with the development puzzle

In a loose historical sequence, as we have seen, the original economic parameters of 'development' gained social attributes, respect for the environment, and for democracy and human rights. Exploring it from these different perspectives provides a sense of its complexity and of the tugs of war pulling in different directions.

It also indicates that answers to the puzzle of how to open up opportunity and reduce marginalization cannot be found by advancing on one front without addressing others: they are all inextricably linked. A multiplicity of efforts on many fronts is more likely to reduce poverty and exploitation than any big-bang theory, mass campaign or set of global resolutions.

The refusal of development to be reduced to a formula upsets anti-poverty enthusiasts, appearing to mire the quest in overlapping layers. But 'development' has always suffered from over-simplification both of problem and prescription. Today, organizations which address single issues – hygiene, child protection, conservation, micro-finance, HIV/AIDS prevention, bonded labor – may be more comprehensible and better-supported than those advocating 'development'.

A continuing problem is that the use of the term is still predominantly economic, and some measurement of economic growth is always present. This helps to reinforce the impression that the neoliberal market-based model with some health and education add-ons is the only one around. Even economically, this paradigm is suspect, since it ignores traditional economies, failing to consider their potential as adaptive bases for their dependents' present and future livelihoods.

This restricted outlook skews the whole picture of what development should be about. The macro-economic version, especially where agriculture and land-holding is concerned, needs to be constantly challenged.

At the opposite end of the spectrum, development as philanthropy also has its limitations. The idea is conveyed to donors that a one-off input – a goat, a toilet – can be the answer in complex socio-political contexts. Expectations are of cost-benefit bonanza and sure-fire success. Attempts to speed things up to get instant results may create dependency on structures not integral to the recipient society. Aid should support an organic process of development, not an artificial substitute.

In the South, people have to live with the term. They experience development on a daily basis in the form of laws, policies, services, projects, administration, jobs and entrepreneurial opportunities. Development goes on all about them in one form or another, even intruding into remote environments and personal and cultural codes once thought unassailable. What many people want is not more of the same, but an end to the damage being done in its name, for which a better contextualized, more inclusive version might prove the antidote

The fashionable synthesis of development into something defined by progress towards measurable human- or environment-related goals begs many questions. The goals omit many predicaments of exclusion, family breakdown, exploitation, the collapse of traditional protective networks and the destruction of once viable ways of life. Instead, we end up with another macro-analysis, garlanded with statistics.

However often it is repeated that there are no universal prescriptions for development, the emphasis on Goals, or campaigns to 'End World Hunger' or 'Make

Poverty History' suggest the opposite. They support the gravitational pull of the idea that the macro level is where development is at and that 'we' in the privileged world can fix up other people's lives in ways they have not envisaged or asked for. In this scenario, the third of humanity living in poverty are players with non-speaking parts in the drama of socio-economic transformation as written by ourselves.

Putting poor people first

The development process advocated by this NoNonsense book is one that helps bring about an empathetic transition from a traditional way of life to one in which choice and opportunity are expanded and health and productivity improved. At the earliest moment, communities themselves should manage the process of engagement with the benefits offered by scientific advance, with legal backing from the state.

The vision may sound idealistic, but there are thousands of locations where it is played out, if one is prepared to settle for incremental and small-scale improvement. Take the community of Lwala in the sugar belt of western Kenya. A number of women who lost their husbands to AIDS have recently taken up market gardening. They grow green leafy kales in the dry season and make deals with local schools to supply produce on a weekly basis. Not only has this paid their daughters' secondary school fees, but it has also improved their diet and helped them start other mini-enterprises: a tree nursery, dairying, rice trading.[4]

What such projects require is modest: instruction in horticulture, small loans, help with the initial marketing deal. These families are not miles off the beaten track, but they are outside the mainstream. Courtesy of a small, well-trained and motivated local NGO team and committed low-level investment, scores of women can transform their eating habits and family prospects. Within years, market gardening around here could take off just as it has elsewhere in Kenya. As long as they manage to hold on to control of their business, then real 'development' will be theirs.

This kind of program starts from where people already are. Improvements derive from existing economic and social realities. The identification of goals, and the means of getting there, are tasks for families and collectives to undertake on their own behalf. Ideas can enter from outside, with increasing ease in the era of the mobile phone. But taking them forward has to come from within.

The task of state-level players is to construct an administrative and legal framework within which this can be done, ensuring that the process of analyzing needs and matching them to practicable strategies for change is undertaken in a democratic way. The job of officials and staff is to see that the provision of resources to implement such plans is equitable and properly carried out.

This version of development respects the reality that local idiosyncrasies govern its prospects in any setting. If there is economic, technological or managerial misfit; if local people see that some intended improvement is too risky; if it can be used by landowners, contractors or officials to exploit local people; if a long list of diverse dynamics are not in favor, the best-laid plans will fail.

Much more investment should therefore be put into micro-planning and implementation at local level, and in building bridges between informal, traditional economies and the modern economy. Exports to earn foreign exchange may also be necessary, but they should not be the paramount concern. The aid and development industry should redesign its machinery to respect the principle that what happens in the local context is central, rather than ornamental, to the grand national plan.

Since people in poor communities make or break efforts on their behalf, organized expressions of their will need to be enlisted in the process. These include organizations in which they have trust – community groups, NGOs, councils and associations. Where these don't exist, they need to be nurtured into being. 'Good governance' and 'decentralization' can be applied to this purpose.

Unfortunately, few political systems champion equitable development. Without leadership which has real claim to authentic popular representation, organic, inclusive and socially cohesive development cannot occur. The business of changing existing structures and insisting on equal rights can only be accomplished in the communities where development has to take place. It would be a huge improvement if the development industry behaved as if this were so.

The international circus

But they don't. Their center of gravity is becoming further and further removed from the scene of action. Ironically, this is partly because there is more aid money available. The bandwagon is inclined to spend the resources on itself.

The donors, including Northern NGOs, prop up the notion that there is such a thing as 'international' development. Certainly there is an international development industry, but that is not the same thing. The international apparatus is vital for regulation of the global commons but its role in designing and implementing development is minimal.

The ever-expanding international circus – conferences, summits, commissions, inquiries into the state of the world's this or that – too often imply that, if only international consensus can be reached around aims and policy principles, the obstacles to development will crumble. Their syntheses of comparative data, the distillation of 'best practice' into thumbnail accounts, convey an impression of progress against difficult odds. They project forward what needs to be done about forests, child prostitution, dams, mining, or public health as if its articulation could bring about a *fait accompli*.

But nothing actually happens internationally to redress poverty and injustice for people.

The idea that it does is an unfortunate mirror-image of its opposite. Undoubtedly, things do happen in international boardrooms and decision-making bodies, which dramatically affect poor people – for the worse. Why is there no symmetry in this equation? Obviously, the framework of national policy greatly affects the path of a country's development, and international prescriptions can exert an influence on that. But what matters far more is whether and how policies are actually put into effect. Many Southern delegates agree to Goals and strategies stipulated at the international level so as to open wide the donor checkbook. They know that circumstances on the ground – social resistance, lack of capacity, refusal by vested interests, costs – mean that they will not be carried out.

Some policy principles agreed to – safeguarding the environment, defending human rights – are exemplary on paper. But their elaboration is so far removed from the experiences of people at the end of the line that it often seems as though local and 'international' development are on different planets.

When you have witnessed the bulldozing of shanty-town dwellings, the brutality of sex work in squalid slums, the rotting garbage heaps picked over by scavenging children, the homes where family upon family recounts the loss of land, livelihood and family pride to make way for 'development', it is impossible not to feel distaste at international policymakers' latter-day discovery of qualities such as 'resilience'.[5] The organizations that reduce key ideas to platitudes also help create the 'enabling' environment in which pauperization occurs. They are able to claim ignorance or lack of responsibility because they have so little understanding of the realities of development in people's lives.

The industry needs to become more responsive and

accountable to the local setting. Less effort should be put into grand international initiatives – 'Marshall Plans for Africa' and long lists of Sustainable Development Goals and targets – and more into making things work on the ground.

In the name of 'the poor'

Since the whole rationale for the development mission is to reduce poverty, it seems legitimate to suggest that more of what is done in the name of 'the poor' should actually be designed to serve them. If one-third of the people on earth have been failed or bypassed, ways should be found to redirect the process.

One way to do this would be to re-emphasize the need for 'participation'. This is a gesture towards inclusion that the international industry only seems able to extend to representatives of civil society who can be invited to workshops at the local Marriott or Sofitel Hotel and will be granted accreditation by the Minister, Regional Governor or Mayor in question. The idea that 'participation' on the ground is what counts has gone into sharp retreat.

The other key to a radical redirection of development efforts is to confer more legitimacy to poor people's existing strategies. Marginalized people are not passive victims. Their success at coping in the face of almost insuperable odds is evidence of resourcefulness. This needs to be taken as a given, not intellectualized as a quality called 'resilience' donors can help them find. Most of them live in an informal economy that needs to be supported, not eclipsed. Destroying that economy in the name of poverty reduction is the worst form of development hypocrisy.

When such things occur, it is understandable that people become equally resourceful at expressing dissent. When the power of their resentment is co-opted by agents of ethnic or religious hatred, the consequences – in Afghanistan, Rwanda, Iraq, Kashmir,

Palestine, northern Nigeria and countless other places – can be devastating. And yes, this is one of the factors threatening world stability, to which the 'war on terror' has been the self-defeating response.

Opposing the one-thought world

In the course of the last 20 years, as the crisis of deteriorating terms of existence has descended around them, some Southern movements have dared to suggest alternatives to the 'one-thought world'.

These are the people in the 21st century who are doing the most to reshape the development mission, whatever it may be called. They are not trying to offer a fully articulated alternative vision to capitalism – an ideological new 'big idea'. They are articulating many visions, redefining and redesigning parameters according to local needs and capacities. And they are trying to create political space in neighborhoods, communities and at the national and international level, to enable these approaches to flourish.

It is easy to dismiss their efforts as a romantic David versus Goliath competition. But the sum of their attempts is the major cause for optimism in the fight to re-inject morality into the development cause. If you go and talk to such people, you will find them reaching out for solidarity, resolute in their determination to defend their rights. 'We will drown, but we will not move,' say people confronted by inundation of their land in India's Narmada Valley.

It is part of the human condition that some people, despite all odds, are courageously prepared to take on forces that to most of us seem unstoppable and monolithic. Their struggle to make the world a better and a fairer place is infinitely worthwhile.

1 See, for example: Gilbert Rist, *The History of Development*; Colin Leys, *The Rise and Fall of Development Theory*; Oswaldo de Rivero, *The Myth of Development*; Wolfgang Sachs, 'Liberating the world from development', *New Internationalist*, 460, Mar 2003; and Jason Hickel, 'The death of international development', *Red Pepper*, Feb 2015. **2** Kate Aldridge in BBC Radio 4's *The Archers*, academic year 2014-2015. **3** Jan Vandemoortele, 'Tackling inequality is key to the post-MDGs development agenda', Feb 2015, nin.tl/tacklinginequality **4** DIG (Development in Gardening) program in western Kenya, personal experience; see reaplifedig.org/our-work/by-country/kenya **5** See, for example, 'Sustaining Human Progress: Reducing Vulnerabilities and Building Resilience', *Human Development Report 2014*, UNDP; hdr.undp.org/en

Index

Page numbers in **bold** refer to main subjects of boxed text.